Labor, Capital, and Growth

Labor, Capital, and Growth

Hans Brems
University of Illinois

Lexington Books
D. C. Heath and Company
Lexington, Massachusetts
Toronto   London

HD
82
.B693

Library of Congress Cataloging in Publication Data

Brems, Hans
Labor, capital, and growth.

1. Economic development—Mathematical models.

I. Title.

HD82.B693   330.9   72–7015

ISBN 0-669-84905-7

Second Printing August 1974.

Published simultaneously in Canada.

Printed in the United States of America.

International Standard Book Number: 0-669-84905-7

Library of Congress Catalog Card Number: 72-7015

To
The Prairie State

Perhaps the most important topic of Political Economy . . . [is] *. . . the progress of a country in wealth and the laws by which the increasing produce is distributed.*

David Ricardo, letter to Malthus of February 23, 1816, *The Works and Correspondence of David Ricardo*, edited by Piero Sraffa, VII, 24.

Contents

List of Figures

List of Tables

Preface

Four years ago I decided to try to write a book putting income distribution, inflation, international trade, and international direct investment squarely into a growth context. Above all, I would try to build a growth model of heterogeneous consumption as well as heterogeneous capital stock—thus seeing within a growth context what economics is supposedly all about, i.e., resource allocation.

Here is the book. It surveys classical, Marxian, linear, and neoclassical models of economic growth. It solves all models explicitly, using elementary mathematics.

I did not succeed in getting beyond steady-state growth but found some comfort in the fact that steady-state growth is a good first approximation to real-world growth. I did succeed in getting beyond balanced growth and have devoted three chapters to unbalanced growth. Nationally as well as internationally, unbalanced growth is also a good first approximation to real-world growth.

Primarily this is a book on theory. But almost all chapters contain references to measurement: Knowledge of empirical orders of magnitude of parameters is often crucial to conclusions reached—and always useful in adding life to the models.

For a reflective fall semester of 1970 as an associate at the University of Illinois Center for Advanced Study, I am indebted to the Graduate College of the University of Illinois. Much of the groundwork was done then.

The contents of this book were first tried out on unsuspecting students at Lunds universitet, Sweden, in the spring of 1970; at home at Illinois in the springs of 1971 and 1972; at the Christian-Albrechts-Universität in Kiel, West Germany, in the summer of 1972; and finally at Göteborgs universitet, Sweden, in the fall of 1972. For their reactions and discussions, I am grateful to my students of Söderslätt, the Prairie, Schleswig-Holstein, and Göta Älv.

For a valuable suggestion I am indebted to Mr. Bojan Popovic, then a graduate student at Illinois. For a grant enabling me to have Mr. Noel Uri check all mathematics used and to have Mr. R. F. McFarlane draw the diagrams, I am indebted to the College of Commerce at the University of Illinois.

The book is dedicated to the Prairie State; here I have so far enjoyed 18 years of happy working conditions.

Urbana, Illinois   Hans Brems

Acknowledgments

Chapters 1 and 6 through 10 are believed to be original, and in some instances such work has been published by the author before. If so, the material has been completely rewritten to fit into this book. The author is indebted to:

(1) The American Economic Association for permission to use, in Chapter 7, material from Hans Brems, "A Growth Model of International Direct Investment," *The American Economic Review*, June 1970, **60**, 320–331.

(2) The Duke University Press for permission to use, in Chapter 1, material from Hans Brems, "Ricardo's Long-Run Equilibrium," *The History of Political Economy*, Fall 1970, **2**, 225–245.

(3) Das Institut für Weltwirtschaft an der Universität Kiel for permission to use, in the appendix to Chapter 3, material from Hans Brems, "Capital Coefficients, Propensities to Save, Calculated and Actual Growth Rates in Eight Countries 1954–1969," *Weltwirtschaftliches Archiv*, Dec. 1972, **108**.

(4) Kyklos-Verlag, Basel, for permission to use, in Chapter 6, material from Hans Brems, "Steady State, Imbalance, and Stability of Two-Country Growth," *Kyklos*, Fasc. 1, 1972, **25**, 49–64.

(5) John Wiley & Sons, Inc., for permission to use, in Chapters 4, 9, and 10, material from Chapters 17, 32, and 48 of Hans Brems, *Quantitative Economic Theory*, New York, London, and Sydney, 1968.

Permission to quote from empirical findings by others was also given generously. The author is indebted to the Harvard University Press and the President and Fellows of Harvard College for permission to use, in Table 5-1, data from H. Barger, "Growth in Developed Nations," *Review of Economics and Statistics*, May 1969, **51**, 143–148, and in Appendix III of Chapter 8, data from P. A. Yotopoulos and L. J. Lau, "A Test for Balanced and Unbalanced Growth," *Review of Economics and Statistics*, Nov. 1970, **52**, 376–384.

Introduction

1. Variables and Parameters

We try to understand economic variables by building models which explain them in terms of something else. That something else presumably is the province either of other sciences such as demography, geology, psychology, physiology, technology, etc., or of public policy. Mathematically, a model is a system of equations containing the variables related to one another through parameters. A parameter is a magnitude fixed by the investigator using information coming from outside the model, such as demographical, geological, psychological, physiological, technological, or public-policy information.

All models presented in this book are solvable—and solved explicitly. By an explicit solution for a variable we mean an equation having that variable alone on one side and nothing but parameters on the other side. Once such a solution has been found, we have understood our variable.

Once such a solution has been found, we are often curious about the direction and strength of the effect exerted upon it by individual parameters. We find that direction and strength by taking the partial derivative of the variable with respect to the parameter (such a partial derivative is sometimes called a multiplier). That it is legitimate to do so follows from the definition of a parameter: Since a parameter is a magnitude fixed by the investigator, it may also be manipulated by him. No such thing could be done to a variable. Variables are solved for within the model, and the solution must be respected. Variables can have their solution value only and can be manipulated only by manipulating the underlying parameters. Since the distinction between variables and parameters is so important, we shall open each of our ten chapters with a list of variables and parameters used in that chapter. The same distinction will now permit us to see the difference between dynamics in the weak and strong sense.

2. Weak and Strong Dynamics

A static system is known to be one in which all variables refer to the same time—hence need not be dated explicitly. From the manipulation of parameters mentioned in Section 1, it is but a short step to think of such manipulation as taking place *over time*. As Walras [6], 318, put it: "In order to make this transition [from the static to the dynamic point of view] we need only suppose the *data* of the problem ... to vary as a function of time."

In other words, we fix a succession of different parameter values over time; but at each particular point of time we still have a system in which all variables refer to the same time—a static system. Such a succession of static systems could be called dynamics in the weak sense.

Dynamics in the weak sense could be likened to a god who remained in full control of the world by fixing personally its parameters at every instant. Such dynamics in the weak sense is found in Ricardian and Marxian economics, to be examined in our Chapters 1 and 2. But what, then, is dynamics in the strong sense?

Suppose one includes in his system either difference equations, relating a variable at one time to a variable at a different time, or differential equations, containing derivatives of variables with respect to time. Since a derivative of a variable with respect to time says something about the way that variable is changing over time, difference and differential equations say essentially the same thing. The presence of either difference or differential equations would make a system dynamic in the strong [2] sense.

Dynamics in the strong sense could be likened to a god who, having fixed once and for all the initial conditions of the world as well as the laws governing its motion, refrains from further interference. Chapters 3 through 10 of this book represent dynamics in the strong sense.

3. Steady-State Growth, Capital Intensity

Define, as Hahn and Matthews [3] did, steady-state growth as stationary proportionate rates of growth of physical outputs. Define capital intensity as capital stock per man hour. Capital widening is then defined as growth under constant capital intensity. Capital deepening, by contrast, is defined as growth under rising capital intensity.

Steady-state growth is, perhaps, a permissible first approximation to real-world growth and is certainly the simplest possible form of dynamics in the strong sense. Capital widening (Chapters 3 and 4) as well as capital deepening (Chapters 5 through 8) may conveniently be examined in their steady-state form. One-sector models (Chapters 3 and 5) as well as multisector models (Chapters 4 and 6 through 10) may also conveniently be examined in their steady-state form.

4. Unbalanced Growth and the Allocation of Resources

Define, as Solow and Samuelson [4] did, balanced growth as identical proportionate rates of growth of physical output for all goods. Real-world growth may be steady-state but is typically unbalanced. Unfortunately most growth models miss imbalance as well as what economics is all about: the allocation of resources.

To allow for imbalance, a growth model needs at least two goods. But to formulate the full allocation problem, it will not do to let the two goods be the consumers' good and the producers' good found in Ricardo, Marx, and the usual [5] two-sector growth models. With only one consumers' good, such models are still models of homogeneous consumption, permitting no substitution among consumers' goods and asking no question, hence offering no answer, concerning the allocation of consumption expenditure among consumers' goods. With only one producers' good, such models are still models of homogeneous capital stock, permitting no substitution among producers' goods and asking no question, hence offering no answer, concerning the allocation of investment expenditure among producers' goods.

A primary purpose of this book is to come to grips with the full allocation of labor, capital, and goods. Expanding the one-good neoclassical model of Chapter 5 into the full-fledged allocation model of Chapter 8 is a difficult job, best done in three steps.

The first step is to borrow a leaf from international-trade theory. Here there are two countries each of which produces one good. International-trade theory has traditionally assumed that neither labor nor capital are free to move internationally. Only goods are free to move: The two goods are substitutes in consumption and are traded internationally. Trade alone constitutes the balance of payments. Chapter 6 solves the only allocation problem arising under such assumptions, i.e., the allocation of consumers' goods between the two countries.

Chapter 7 takes the second step towards a full-fledged allocation model by letting capital move internationally in the form of international direct investment. An additional allocation problem now arises: How do a country's entrepreneurs allocate their investment between domestic parent firm and foreign subsidiary? Chapter 7 solves this problem by assuming that the entrepreneurs allocate investment such as to maximize the present worth of all their future profits.

Chapter 8 takes the third and final step towards a full-fledged allocation model by abandoning the international economy and returning to a national one. Within a national economy, labor and capital are free to move among industries. Within our national economy each of two goods are assumed to serve interchangeably as a consumers' or as a producers' good. As a result, there will be four distinct capital stocks and four distinct investment flows in our two-good economy. There will be a fourfold interaction between its two industries: First, the two industries compete in their demand for labor. In the labor market they must pay the same money wage rate. Second, the two industries compete in their demand for investment goods. In the market for each good they must pay the same price for it. Third, the two industries compete in their demand for money capital. In the money-capital market the capitalist-entrepreneurs allocate their savings between the two industries such as to maximize the present worth of all their future profits. Fourth, the two industries compete in their supply of consumers' goods. In the consumers' goods market the two goods are good, but not perfect, substitutes, and each consumer has a taste for both of them. All this may sound like general-equilibrium theory. But ordinary general-equilibrium theory is static; ours is cast in a growth setting.

5. Embodied Technological Progress

Chapters 3 and 4 assumed technological progress to be absent, and Chapters 5 through 8 assumed it to be present only in disembodied form. Much technological progress, however, makes its way into the economy in the form of new and physically different hardware—as Ricardo observed, cf. our Chapter 1, Section 5! Our Chapters 9 and 10 assume that under steady technological progress no retired producers' good will be replaced by another unit physically identical to it. It will be replaced by a new and different one, and not until this happens can technological progress be exploited.

Thus the replacement decision becomes crucial to growth theory. Chapter 9 will develop a pure theory of the replacement decision within a firm. From that theory Chapter 10 will derive a vintage model of growth. In such a model, a low rate of interest encourages firms to adopt short useful lives of durable producers' goods, thus staying close to the fringe of known technology. This phenomenon has aptly been called "capital quickening."

6. Organization

In its survey of classical, Marxian, linear, and neoclassical models of economic growth, the book will proceed from the simple to the complicated, gradually coming to grips with its subject matter. Yet each chapter is self-contained and may be read without reading any other. The only exception is Chapter 10 which has Chapter 9 for a prerequisite.

Notes

[1] Denison, E. F., *Why Growth Rates Differ*, Washington, D.C., 1967, Ch. 16.

[2] Frisch, R., "Propagation and Impulse Problems in Dynamic Economics," *Economic Essays in Honour of Gustav Cassel*, London 1933, 171.

[3] Hahn, F. H., and R. C. O. Matthews, "The Theory of Economic Growth: A Survey," *Econ. Jour.*, Dec. 1964, **74,** 779–902.

[4] Solow, R. M., and P. A. Samuelson, "Balanced Growth under Constant Returns to Scale," *Econometrica*, July 1953, **21,** 412–424.

[5] Uzawa, H., "On a Two-Sector Model of Economic Growth," I-II, *Rev. Econ. Stud.*, Oct. 1961, **29,** 40–47 and June 1963, **30,** 105–118.

[6] Walras, L., *Elements of Pure Economics*, Homewood, Ill., 1954.

[7] Yotopoulos, P. A., and L. J. Lau, "A Test for Balanced and Unbalanced Growth," *Rev. Econ. Stat.,* Nov. 1970, **52,** 376–384.

I. Capital and Immiserization

1 Ricardo on Machinery

Relevance rather than reverence makes it appropriate to begin our survey of labor, capital, and growth with another look at Ricardo: With his emphasis on an expanding population swallowing up any gains in individual standards of living, his model qualifies as a tool of analysis of an underdeveloped economy. With his emphasis on irreproducible nature, his model qualifies as a tool of analysis of an industrialized economy becoming increasingly conscious of what it is doing to nature.

Let us set out Ricardo's long-run model mathematically and let us remember to include his fixed capital in the form of durable producers' goods—treated erroneously, we think, in an early mathematization of Ricardo [11] and excluded from the two most refined recent ones [4] and [6].[a] Meeting Ricardo on his own ground, we shall find much of his pessimism unfounded.

1. Notation

Variables

$H \equiv$ revenue *minus* operating labor cost
$I \equiv$ output of producers' goods
$J \equiv$ present net worth of an investment project
$L \equiv$ labor employed
$P \equiv$ price of consumers' goods
$p \equiv$ price of producers' goods
$S \equiv$ physical capital stock of producers' goods
$w \equiv$ money wage rate
$X \equiv$ output of consumers' goods

---

[a] Whewell's model has two sections on fixed capital, [11], 174-176 and 179. But as I [1] have tried to demonstrate, his concepts of net income from and depreciation of fixed capital are inconsistent with a Ricardian economy. In their highly refined mathematical models, neither Samuelson [6] nor Pasinetti [4] incorporated durable producers' goods, hence did not examine the effects of technological improvements of such goods. Pasinetti's model did have two goods in it, but they were corn and gold.

Parameters

$a_1 \equiv$ labor required to produce one physical unit of producers' goods
$a_2 \equiv$ labor required to operate one physical unit of producers' goods
$\beta, \gamma \equiv$ exponents of production function
$e \equiv$ Euler's number, the base of natural logarithms
$M \equiv$ multiplicative factor of production function
$N \equiv$ nature
$r \equiv$ rate of interest
$u \equiv$ useful life of producers' goods

The symbol m, to be defined in Eq. (8), stands for an agglomeration of parameters. The symbol t is the time coordinate. All flow variables refer to the instantaneous rate of that variable measured on a per annum basis.

2. The Equations of the Model

The Ricardian model has two industries in it, a producers' and a consumers' goods industry, called 1 and 2, respectively.

The producers' goods industry produces tools and implements used by farmers and is delightfully simple: Its production function has only one input in it, i.e., labor. Let a_1 be the labor required to produce one physical unit of producers' goods, then

(1) $$L_1 = a_1 I$$

where a_1 is a technological parameter. Let there be pure competition and freedom of entry and exit in the producers' goods industry, then the price of producers' goods will equal their cost of production per unit:

(2) $$p = a_1 w$$

The consumers' goods industry is farming and is less simple: Its production function has three inputs in it, labor, durable producers' goods, and nature, called "land." Let a_2 be the labor required to operate one physical unit of producers' goods, then

(3) $$L_2 = a_2 S$$

In one sense Ricardo was a marginalist, in another he was not. The coefficient a_2 being a technological parameter, the number of physical units of producers' goods applied could not be varied without varying labor in the same proportion, and in this sense Ricardo was not a marginalist. A bundle of a_2 labor *plus* one physical unit of producers' goods was called "a portion of capital," and the number of portions of capital applied to a given piece of land could be varied. In this sense Ricardo was a marginalist. When farmers applied more portions of capital to a given piece of land, output would rise but by decreasing increments. Let us simulate that relationship by the linearly homogeneous production function

(4) $$X = MS^\beta N^\gamma$$

where $0 < \beta < 1; 0 < \gamma < 1; \beta + \gamma = 1; M > 0;$ and $N > 0$. X and S are variables, M and N parameters.

Since durable producers' goods appear among the inputs of the production function (4), dynamic planning is appropriate. In dynamic planning, the present net worth of an investment project is maximized. On a given piece of land, let a Ricardian farmer consider acquiring a capital stock of S new physical units of producers' goods in order to produce an output of X consumers' goods to be sold at the price P, a parameter to the purely competitive farmer. Revenue is then PX. Since a_2 was the labor required to operate one physical unit of producers' goods, and w was the money wage rate, operating labor cost is a_2wS. Revenue *minus* operating labor cost is

(5) $$H \equiv PX - a_2wS$$

The present worth of revenue *minus* operating labor cost per small fraction dt of a year located t years away in the future is

$$He^{-rt}\, dt$$

where e is Euler's number, the base of natural logarithms, and where r is the rate of interest, assumed to be positive. The rate of interest r represents the cost of money capital to the farmer and is assumed not to vary with the amount of money he needs.

The present gross worth of the investment project is defined as the sum total of revenue *minus* operating labor cost over the entire useful life u of the new physical units of producers' goods:

$$\int_0^u He^{-rt}\, dt = H\frac{1 - e^{-ru}}{r}$$

Let p be the price of a new physical unit of producers' goods. Assume the salvage value of the unit when retired to be zero. The present net worth of the investment project is defined as the sum total of revenue *minus* operating labor cost over the entire useful life u of the new physical units of producers' goods *minus* the cost of acquiring them:

$$J \equiv H\frac{1 - e^{-ru}}{r} - pS$$

Insert (2) and (5) and write present net worth as

(6)
$$J = (PX - a_2 wS) \frac{1 - e^{-ru}}{r} - a_1 wS$$

How large is the capital stock S which maximizes present net worth (6)? The first-order condition for a present-net-worth maximum is that the derivative of (6) with respect to S be zero. Use (4) to carry out the derivation and find

(7)
$$S = \left(\frac{m}{\beta M N^\gamma} \frac{w}{P} \right)^{-1/\gamma}$$

where

(8)
$$m \equiv \frac{a_1 r}{1 - e^{-ru}} + a_2$$

The second-order condition for a present-net-worth maximum is that the second derivative of (6) with respect to S

$$\frac{d^2 J}{dS^2} = \beta(\beta - 1)MPS^{\beta-2}N^\gamma \frac{1 - e^{-ru}}{r} < 0$$

which it is, because $0 < \beta < 1$. So much for the theory of the firm.

The real wage rate w/P must, in the long run, be high enough to "enable the labourers, one with another, to subsist and to perpetuate their race, without either increase or diminution" [5], 93. If the real wage rate were higher than this subsistence minimum, population would rise and thereby depress the real wage rate. And if the real wage rate were lower than this subsistence minimum, population would fall and thus raise the real wage rate. Before we dismiss such a population equilibrium, we should ponder the present population explosion in the underdeveloped world! To Ricardo, then, while the money wage rate w and the price of consumers' goods P are variables, the real wage rate w/P is a parameter.

But just as the Ricardian system has a long-run horizontal supply curve of labor, it has one for capital as well:[b] "The farmer and manufacturer can no more live without profit than the labourer without wages" [5], 122. If the rate of profit were higher than "an adequate compensation for their trouble, and the risk which they must necessarily encounter in employing their capital productively," accumulation would rise and depress the rate. And if the rate

[b] Samuelson [6] agrees that Ricardo's system has a horizontal supply curve for capital and entrepreneurship. Schumpeter [7] considers such an interpretation as merely one among several possible ones.

were lower than that minimum, accumulation would fall and thus raise the rate. Let the rate of interest r representing the cost of money capital to the firm, used above, be that minimum. To Ricardo, then, the rate of interest r is a parameter.

Aggregate employment equals the sum of labor employed in the two industries:

$$(9) \qquad L \equiv L_1 + L_2$$

In a stationary economy with useful life of producers' goods being u and their age distribution being even, each year $1/u$ of the stock of producers' goods is retired and must be replaced, hence

$$(10) \qquad I = \frac{S}{u}$$

3. Solution for Sustainable Labor Force

Insert (1), (3), (7), and (10) into (9) and solve for sustainable labor force

$$(11) \qquad L = \left(\frac{a_1}{u} + a_2\right)\left(\frac{m}{\beta M N^\gamma}\frac{w}{P}\right)^{-1/\gamma}$$

where m stands for (8). Here, then, is the total sustainable labor force expressed in terms of parameters alone. The labor force (11) is sustainable in the sense that it will sustain itself at subsistence minimum as well as ensure the farmers a normal rate of interest on their capital.

Could Ricardo draw any policy conclusions from this great achievement of his macroeconomics? Towards the end of his Chapter 5 on wages he warned against all social-security schemes:[c] If public policy tried to make the economy support a labor force in excess of the sustainable one, only unemployment and starvation could result—a conclusion earning economics the label of "dismal science"!

Quite a different matter it was that technological progress might enlarge the sustainable labor force. Such progress represented the only hope within the Ricardian system, and it becomes urgent for us to see if Ricardo's own pessimism with respect to such progress was justified. To that question we shall now turn and show that it is ultimately an empirical one.

---

[c] Social-security schemes were pioneered in an atmosphere not contaminated by classical— or any other—economic theory, i.e., the atmosphere of Bismarck's *Reich*.

4. Disembodied Technological Progress

Within the Ricardian system a clear distinction is made between disembodied and embodied technological progress. The former is exemplified by [5], 80:

"...If, by the introduction of a course of turnips, I can feed my sheep besides raising my corn, the land on which the sheep were before fed becomes unnecessary, and the same quantity of raw produce is raised by the employment of a less quantity of land."

This is precisely the kind of technological progress nowadays called disembodied and represented by the growth of the multiplicative factor M in the production function (4) above. How does such progress affect total sustainable labor force L? The elasticity of L with respect to M appears immediately from (11):

$$(12) \qquad \frac{\partial L}{\partial M} \frac{M}{L} = \frac{1}{\gamma}$$

Since $0 < \gamma < 1$ this elasticity is positive: Disembodied technological progress will raise sustainable labor force. This agrees with Ricardo: Such improvements "give a great stimulus to population" [5], 81n.

5. Embodied Technological Progress

Ricardo then turns to a very different kind of technological progress [5], 82:

"Such improvements ... are rather directed to the formation of the capital applied to the land, than to the cultivation of the land itself. Improvements in agricultural implements, such as the plough and the thrashing machine ... are of this nature."

This is embodied technological progress, and it may take two alternative forms. First, it may reduce the labor a_1 required to *produce* one physical unit of producers' goods. Reducing a_1 can be seen as an example of process innovation within the producers' goods industry: The same quality of producer's goods may now be produced with less input per unit of output.

Second, embodied technological progress may reduce the labor a_2 required to *operate* one physical unit of producers' goods. Reducing a_2 can be seen as an example of product innovation within the producers' goods industry: With the same input per unit of output, a higher quality of producers' goods may now be produced—higher quality in the sense of being more automatic, thus requiring less labor to operate it.

The effect of product innovation reducing a_2 was examined in Ricardo's numerical example in Chapter 31 "On Machinery" [5], 388–390. Here, by acquiring machines of a newly invented kind valued at £7500, Ricardo's capitalist-entrepreneur may reduce his wage bill from £13,000 to £5500. Thus the number of machines is up.

We fully agree: It is very clear what will happen to the optimal capital stock S. Both improvements, whether reducing a_1 or a_2, represent reductions of m as defined by (8), and the elasticity of S with respect to m appears immediately from (7):

$$13) \qquad \frac{\partial S}{\partial m} \frac{m}{S} = -\frac{1}{\gamma}$$

Since $0 < \gamma < 1$ this elasticity is negative: Embodied technological progress, whether reducing a_1 or a_2, will raise optimal capital stock. But what will it do to sustainable labor force? Here, two forces are at work in opposite directions: While the number of physical units of producers' goods S is up, it now takes less labor to either build (a_1) or operate (a_2) each physical unit.

By the time Ricardo was writing the third edition of his *Principles* there was little doubt in his mind. In his newly added Chapter 31 he elaborated the dire consequences of embodied technological progress, expressing himself quite categorically [5], 390:

"...there will necessarily be a diminution in the demand for labour, population will become redundant, and the situation of the labouring classes will be that of distress and poverty."

Agreeing with the philosophy, if not the practice, of Ned Ludd, Ricardo concluded [5], 392:

"...that the opinion entertained by the labouring class, that the employment of machinery is frequently detrimental to their interests, is not founded on prejudice and error, but is conformable to the correct principles of political economy."

Harboring prejudice and error, we do not agree: Let us go back to our solution for total sustainable labor force (11) and find its elasticities with respect to a_1 and a_2:

$$(14) \qquad \frac{\partial L}{\partial a_1} \frac{a_1}{L} = -\frac{(ru + e^{-ru} - 1)a_2/(1 - e^{-ru}) + \beta m}{(a_1/u + a_2)\gamma m} \frac{a_1}{u}$$

$$(15) \qquad \frac{\partial L}{\partial a_2} \frac{a_2}{L} = -\frac{[(1 - e^{-ru})/ru - \gamma]ra_1/(1 - e^{-ru}) + \beta a_2}{(a_1/u + a_2)\gamma m} a_2$$

What are the signs of these two elasticities?

16

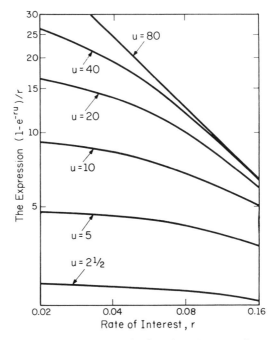

Figure 1-1. Mapping the function $(1 - e^{-ru})/r$.

The first elasticity (14) is easy: A table of powers of e will show that $ru + e^{-ru} - 1$ is positive for any $ru > 0$, hence under the assumptions made, (14) is unequivocally negative: Embodied technological progress reducing the labor a_1 required to produce one physical unit of producers' goods, will raise sustainable labor force.

The second elasticity (15) is less easy: A part of the numerator, i.e., the bracket, could be negative. Let us examine the sign of that bracket within empirically plausible ranges of the values of our parameters γ, r, and u.

As for r, Kuznets [2], 421, found the rate of return on corporate assets to be 0.13 and 0.06 in underdeveloped and developed economies, respectively. These values are on the high side, because the return on noncorporate assets is lower than on corporate ones.

As for u, the U.S. Department of Commerce [8], [9] estimates useful lives of structures and equipment to be from 20 to 30 years in the United States. On underdeveloped economies, Kuznets is silent.

Figure 1-1 maps the fundamental function $(1 - e^{-ru})/r$ for rather wide ranges of r and u. For slightly narrower ranges, Table 1-1 shows the values of γ required to make the bracket of the numerator of (15) positive.

Table 1-1. Values of γ Required to
Make Bracket of (15) Nonnegative

r	u	$\gamma \leq$ $(1 - e^{-ru})/ru =$
0.04	20	0.69
0.04	40	0.50
0.08	20	0.50
0.08	40	0.30
0.16	20	0.30
0.16	40	0.16

What is known about the order of magnitude of γ, the elasticity of output with respect to land? In his survey of agricultural Cobb-Douglas production functions for underdeveloped and developed economies, Walters [10], 32–33, found few γ's higher than $\frac{1}{2}$ and most around $\frac{1}{4}$.

Let it be permissible to conclude from the distributive shares to the exponents of an aggregate Cobb-Douglas production function. Then in developed economies γ must be far less than $\frac{1}{4}$: Nordhaus and Tobin [3], 61–64, summarized Denison findings to the effect that in the United States, land's share declined from 9 to 3 per cent from 1900 to 1950. They considered a land's share of 0.05 one of their "stylized" facts. In underdeveloped economies γ must still be somewhat less than $\frac{1}{4}$: Kuznets [2], 421, found the share of income from material assets, defined as land *plus* reproducible assets, to be around $\frac{1}{4}$ in such economies.

We conclude that in the first five cases examined in Table 1-1 γ easily meets the requirements posed. Only the sixth case, in which $r = 0.16$ and $u = 40$, requires a γ less than $\frac{1}{4}$. While in underdeveloped economies the rate of return to capital may be as high as 0.16, useful life is unlikely to be as long as 40 years. And even if it were, there is in the numerator of (15) still the term βa_2 to go, and in underdeveloped economies producers' goods are, perhaps, less automatic and therefore have a higher a_2 than those of developed economies. As a result, the possibility of a negative numerator of (15) must be remote.

We expect, then, the second elasticity (15) to be negative: Embodied technological progress reducing the labor a_2 required to operate one physical unit of producers' goods, will raise sustainable labor force.

6. Conclusion

We have examined Ricardo's problem of the effects of technological progress upon sustainable labor force. To underdeveloped economies, this problem is the most important of all the Ricardian problems. We have found no flaw in Ricardo's logic. Whether or not his pessimistic prediction of those effects is correct is ultimately an empirical problem. We, who have so much more and better data than he had, do not think that the elasticity γ of output with respect to land is actually high enough to justify his pessimism.

Notes

[1] Brems, H., "Ricardo's Long-Run Equilibrium," *Hist. Pol. Econ.*, Fall 1970, **2**, 225–245.

[2] Kuznets, S., *Modern Economic Growth, Rate, Structure, and Spread*, New Haven and London, 1966.

[3] Nordhaus, W., and J. Tobin, "Is Growth Obsolete?" *Fiftieth Anniversary Colloquium V by the National Bureau of Economic Research*, New York, 1972, 1–80.

[4] Pasinetti, L. L., "A Mathematical Formulation of the Ricardian System," *Rev. Econ. Stud.*, Feb. 1960, **27**, 78–98.

[5] Ricardo, D., *The Principles of Political Economy and Taxation*, reproduced in *The Works and Correspondence of David Ricardo*, P. Sraffa and M. H. Dobb (eds.), New York, 1951.

[6] Samuelson, P. A., "A Modern Treatment of the Ricardian Economy," *Quart. Jour. Econ.*, Feb. and May, 1959, **73**, 1–35 and 217–231.

[7] Schumpeter, J. A., *History of Economic Analysis*, New York, 1954.

[8] U.S. Department of Commerce, Office of Business Economics, "New Estimates of Fixed Business Capital in the United States, 1925–65," *Surv. Curr. Bus.*, Dec. 1966, **46**, 34–40.

[9] U.S. Department of Commerce, Office of Business Economics, "Fixed Business Capital in the United States, 1925–68," *Surv. Curr. Bus.*, Feb. 1969, **49**, 20–27.

[10] Walters, A. A., "Production and Cost Functions: An Econometric Survey," *Econometrica*, Jan.–Apr. 1963, **31**, 1–66.

[11] Whewell, W., "Mathematical Exposition of Some of the Leading Doctrines in Mr. Ricardo's 'Principles of Political Economy and Taxation'," *Transactions of the Cambridge Philosophical Society*, 1833, **4**, 155–198.

2 Marx: Model Versus Prediction

Following Samuelson [5], we concentrate on Marx, the theorist interested in the long-run working mechanism of capitalism. We ignore Marx the historian, the sociologist, the pamphleteer, and the labor organizer.

Like Quesnay [4], Marx [3] saw the general interdependence of industries. His simplest model has two industries in it, a producers' and a consumers' goods industry. Unlike Ricardo, Marx uses fixed input-output coefficients. Consequently, there are no diminishing returns to anything, and within a constant technology there is no substitution between labor and capital. Inputs are the services of producers' goods and labor, and both industries use both inputs. The useful life of producers' goods is one year, so in a stationary economy the stock of producers' goods existing at a moment of time equals the output per annum of such goods. The period of production is also one year: Input of the services of producers' goods and labor generates output one year later. Since, however, in a stationary economy everything repeats itself year after year, it is unnecessary to date our variables.

1. Notation

Variables

$L \equiv$ labor employed
$P \equiv$ price of good
$r \equiv$ rate of interest
$S_i \equiv$ ith industry's physical capital stock
$w \equiv$ money wage rate
$X \equiv$ physical output

Parameters

$a \equiv$ labor coefficient
$b \equiv$ capital coefficient

Subscripts $i = 1, 2$ refer to industry number. All flow variables refer to the instantaneous rate of that variable measured on a per annum basis.

2. The Equations of the Model

Like the Ricardian model, the Marxian one has two industries in it, a producers' and a consumers' goods industry, to be called 1 and 2, respectively.
Aggregate employment equals the sum of labor employed in the two industries:

(1) $$L \equiv L_1 + L_2$$

Because producers' goods have a useful life of one year, the output of
producers' goods per annum equals the sum of physical capital stocks
existing in the two industries:

(2) $$X_1 = S_1 + S_2$$

Labor input and physical capital stocks are in proportion to output:

(3), (4) $$L_i = a_i X_i$$

(5), (6) $$S_i = b_i X_i$$

Both industries use both[a] inputs, so $a_i > 0$ and $b_i > 0$. Under pure
competition, freedom of entry and exit, and absence of uncertainty, each
industry breaks even: Revenue equals cost with interest added to it at the
rate r for one year—the period of production was assumed to be one year.
The rate r is the same in the two industries, or capital would leave the low-rate
industry and enter the high-rate industry until the two rates were equal—as
Marx saw in his Volume III:[b]

(7) $$P_1 X_1 = (1 + r)(wL_1 + P_1 S_1)$$

(8) $$P_2 X_2 = (1 + r)(wL_2 + P_1 S_2)$$

3. Rate of Interest and the Real Wage Rate

Marx' preoccupation was with the Law of Immiserization: Capitalism
would generate misery and unrest and would eventually be overthrown by
the proletariat.

Marx did not say unequivocally that the real wage rate would fall. He did
say unequivocally that when capital accumulation goes on, as it must, the

---

[a] This is a realistic improvement on Ricardo although, as we know [1], in the United States
the producers' goods industry has a much lower capital intensity than the consumers' goods
industry.

[b] But not in Volume I. On the relationship between Volumes I and III, see Samuelson [6],
[7].

rate of interest would fall. Consequently, there are three questions before us: First, within Marx' model, how are the rate of interest and the real wage rate related under stationary technology? Second, how are they related under technological progress? Third, quite apart from Marx' model, what does the history of capitalism teach us?

4. Stationary Technology

Within Marx' model, how are the rate of interest and the real wage rate related under stationary technology?

Divide (7) and (8) by X_1 and X_2, respectively, use (3) through (6), find a system of two equations in the three variables w, P_1 and P_2, and solve it for the real wage rate

(9) $$\frac{w}{P_2} = \frac{1/(1 + r) - b_1}{a_1 b_2(1 + r) + a_2[1 - b_1(1 + r)]}$$

Let us make the eminently realistic assumptions that the rate of interest r and the factor $1 - b_1(1 + r)$ are positive. Hence the real wage rate is positive.

To interpret (9), take the derivative of it with respect to $1 + r$ and find

(10) $$\frac{\partial(w/P_2)}{\partial(1 + r)} = -\frac{a_2[1 - b_1(1 + r)]^2 + a_1 b_2(1 + r)[2 - b_1(1 + r)]}{(1 + r)^2 D^2}$$

where D is the denominator of (9). What is the sign of (10)? As we saw, Marx assumed both industries to use both inputs, so $a_i > 0$ and $b_i > 0$. Furthermore, we just assumed the rate of interest r and the factor $1 - b_1(1 + r)$ to be positive. Hence the derivative (10) is unequivocally negative: Within a stationary technology the rate of interest and the real wage rate must always move in opposite directions: The rate of interest can come down only if the real wage rate goes up.

5. Technological Progress

Within Marx' model, how are the rate of interest and the real wage rate related under technological progress?

Suppose that the capitalist-entrepreneur feels somehow forced to adopt a new technology, although it offers him a lower rate of interest than he was earning before the new technology came along. Capitalist-entrepreneurs have been heard lamenting such misfortune! What *is* forcing him? If the capitalist-entrepreneur is adopting the new technology rather than sticking to the old one, it must be because something has reduced his rate of interest under the original technology even more. What is that something? It follows from the negativity of (10) that if under the original technology the rate of interest is down, the real wage rate is up. Once adopted by the majority of the capitalist-entrepreneurs, the new technology has depressed the price of consumers' goods P_2 and raised the real wage rate w/P_2. The remaining capitalist-entrepreneurs will have no choice: They, too, will have to adopt the new technology. The good old days will never be back.

In conclusion, even under technological progress the rate of interest can come down only if the real wage rate goes up. Within Marx' model, then, it is difficult to see where the misery and unrest could come from. To be true, Ricardian diminishing returns could have helped Marx establish his Law of Immiserization, but that particular part of the Ricardian system Marx did not accept. Mathematical training might have helped Marx see what he was doing, but his legal and philosophical education provided no such training.

6. History

What does the history of capitalism teach us? For the United States 1900/1909–1949/1957, Kravis [2] found the rate of interest to have remained stationary, but wage in 1929 prices per man hour to have been growing at an average proportionate rate of 0.025 per annum. To such historical facts—well simulated by neoclassical growth models pioneered by Tinbergen [9] and Solow [8]—we shall return in Chapter 5.

Notes

[1] Gordon, R. A., "Differential Changes in the Prices of Consumers' and Capital Goods," *Am. Econ. Rev.*, Dec. 1961, **51,** 937–957.

[2] Kravis, I. B., "Relative Income Shares in Fact and Theory," *Am. Econ. Rev.*, Dec. 1959, **49,** 917–949.

[3] Marx, K., *Capital*, I-III, Moscow and London, 1954, 1957, and 1962.

[4] Quesnay, F., *Tableau économique*, Versailles, 1758.

[5] Samuelson, P. A., "Wages and Interest: A Modern Dissection of Marxian Economic Models," *Am. Econ. Rev.*, Dec. 1957, **47,** 884–912.

[6] Samuelson, P. A., "Understanding the Marxian Notion of Exploitation: A Summary of the So-Called Transformation Problem Between Marxian Values and Competitive Prices," *Jour. Econ. Lit.*, June 1971, **9,** 399–431.

[7] Samuelson, P. A., "The Economics of Marx: An Ecumenical Reply," *Jour. Econ. Lit.*, March 1972, **10,** 51–57.

[8] Solow, R. M., "A Contribution to the Theory of Economic Growth," *Quart. Jour. Econ.*, Feb. 1956, **70,** 65–94.

[9] Tinbergen, J., "Zur Theorie der langfristigen Wirtschaftsentwicklung," *Weltw. Archiv*, May 1942, **55,** 511–549.

II. Capital Widening

3 Harrod-Domar Steady-State Growth

Ricardian and Marxian economics represent what we have called dynamics in the weak sense: Ricardo and Marx fixed a succession of different parameter values over time, but at each particular point of time all variables referred to the same time. We likened dynamics in the weak sense to a god who remained in full control of the world by fixing personally its parameters at every instant.

By assuming that households save and firms invest, Keynes was feeling his way towards dynamics in the strong sense. But he never made it. Confining himself to an ultrashort run, Keynes treated net investment as positive, yet failed to consider its effect upon capital stock. Had a longer run been considered, a positive net investment would have expanded capital stock. Such an expansion would have found its mathematical expression in a differential equation like (6) below, and the presence of such a differential equation would have made the Keynesian system dynamic in the strong sense—and would have reversed some cherished Keynesian conclusions. We likened dynamics in the strong sense to a god who, having fixed once and for all the initial conditions of the world as well as the laws governing its motion, refrained from further interference.

Dynamics in the strong sense was offered by Cassel [2], Lundberg [8], Domar [3], and Harrod [5]. The Cassel-Lundberg-Harrod-Domar growth model was an aggregative one: Entrepreneurs produce a single good from labor and an immortal capital stock of that good, hence investment is the act of setting aside part of output for installation as capital stock. Capital stock is the result of accumulated savings under an autonomously given propensity to save, and available labor force is growing autonomously. There is no substitution between labor and capital, and technology is stationary.

1. Notation

Variables

$C \equiv$ consumption
$g_v \equiv$ proportionate rate of growth of the variable v where $v \equiv C, I, L, S,$ and X

$I \equiv$ investment
$L \equiv$ labor employed
$S \equiv$ physical capital stock
$X \equiv$ physical output

Parameters

$a \equiv$ labor coefficient
$b \equiv$ capital coefficient
$c \equiv$ propensity to consume
$g_F \equiv$ proportionate rate of growth of available labor force F
$F \equiv$ available labor force

The parameters listed are stationary except F, whose time path is governed by the stationary growth rate g_F. For time coordinate we use t. All flow variables refer to the instantaneous rate of that variable measured on a per annum basis.

2. The Equations of the Model

Five variable growth rates are listed in Section 1. To all apply the definition

(1) through (5)
$$g_v \equiv \frac{dv}{dt} \frac{1}{v}$$

Define investment as the derivative of capital stock with respect to time

(6)
$$I \equiv \frac{dS}{dt}$$

Exactly as they were in the Marxian model, let labor input as well as capital stock be in proportion to output:

(7)
$$L = aX$$

(8)
$$S = bX$$

where $a > 0$ and $b > 0$. Let consumption be a fixed proportion of output:

(9)
$$C = cX$$

where $0 < c < 1$. Output equilibrium requires output to equal the sum of consumption and investment demand for it, or inventory would either accumulate or be depleted:

(10)
$$X = C + I$$

3. Solutions for Proportionate Rates of Growth

Use (1) through (6) and (8) through (10) to find

(11)
$$g_X = \frac{1 - c}{b}$$

So the proportionate rate of growth of output equals the propensity to save divided by the capital coefficient. Since both $1 - c$ and b are stationary parameters, the proportionate rate of growth of output is stationary, hence growth is steady-state.

Succeeding in doing what Keynes had failed to do, the Harrod-Domar model reversed one Keynesian conclusion: In a truncated Keynesian model, a lower propensity to save could not hurt investment, for the latter was a parameter, but would expand output. Consequently, saving was a bad thing, and the less of it the better for an underemployed economy. By contrast, a lower propensity to save can hurt Harrod-Domar investment, for the latter is now a variable permitting growth, hence a lower propensity to save reduces the rate of growth. Saving, then, is a good thing, and the less of it the worse for a growing economy.

Use (1) through (5) upon (6) through (9) and find the solutions for the remaining proportionate rates of growth in our system:

(12)
$$g_C = g_X$$

(13)
$$g_I = g_X$$

(14)
$$g_L = g_X$$

(15)
$$g_S = g_X$$

4. Underemployment, Full Employment, or Labor Shortage?

One Keynesian conclusion still holds in a Harrod-Domar model: There is no mechanism ensuring a feasible solution for output, i.e., that employment is less than or equal to available labor force:

(16)
$$L \leq F$$

Feasibility will have to be ensured by assumption, then. But even if that were done for some particular time, no mechanism would ensure continued feasibility in the sense that

(17)
$$g_L \leq g_F$$

If $g_L > g_F$ there would be an ever-rising labor shortage; if $g_L = g_F$ there would be continued feasibility; if $g_L < g_F$ there would be an ever-rising unemployment.

5. Instability

By stability of equilibrium we mean the ability of equilibrium to restore itself after a disturbance. Let an asterisk denote disequilibrium values. Let entrepreneurs make the mistake of expecting demand for output to be growing by $*g_X \equiv \lambda g_X$ where $0 < \lambda < 1$ or $\lambda > 1$. To avoid inventory change they will then plan for output to be growing at $*g_X$. To maintain the stationary capital-output ratio b according to (8), they will plan for capital stock to be growing at $*g_S = *g_X$. According to (6), investment will then be

$$(18) \qquad *I = *g_S S = *g_X S = \lambda g_X S$$

Add (9) and (18), use (8) and (11), and write aggregate demand

$$(19) \qquad C + *I = [c + \lambda(1 - c)]X$$

If $0 < \lambda < 1$, aggregate demand will fall short of output, inventory will accumulate, and entrepreneurs will plan to lower the proportionate rate of growth even further. If $\lambda > 1$, aggregate demand will be in excess of output, inventory will be depleted, and entrepreneurs will plan to raise the proportionate rate of growth even further. The initial mistake, then, is self-magnifying rather than self-correcting. Once the Harrod-Domar economy is pushed, however slightly, off its equilibrium growth path, it is doomed to keep veering away from that path.

6. Empirical Orders of Magnitude

Our appendix offers empirical estimates of the Harrod-Domar capital coefficient b and propensity to save $1 - c$.

Appendix:
Empirical
Measurements

1. Introduction

One the eve of its changeover to a new system of national accounts, the OECD brought together in one volume [10] comparable and consistent national accounts for its member countries 1953–1969. Let us use this volume to estimate Harrod-Domar capital coefficients and propensities to save for eight advanced[a] countries. Let us use the estimates to calculate the Harrod-Domar growth rate according to (11). Finally, let us confront the calculated with the actual growth rate.

2. Capital Coefficients

What the capital coefficient b is used for in the Harrod-Domar model is the derivation from its Eqs. (6) and (8) of the investment function

$$(20) \qquad I = b \frac{dX}{dt}$$

It follows from Eq. (6) that Harrod-Domar investment I is *net* investment and from Eq. (10) that Harrod-Domar output X is *net* output. Consequently use Part Three, Table 2, lines 3, 8, and 17 of the OECD accounts [10] to define

$I \equiv$ net domestic fixed asset formation $\equiv$ gross domestic fixed asset formation at 1963 prices (line 3) *minus* depreciation and other operating provisions at 1963 prices (line 17).

$X \equiv$ net national product $\equiv$ gross national product at 1963 market prices (line 8) *minus* depreciation and other operating provisions at 1963 prices (line 17).

$\Delta X \equiv$ annual increments of X.

In Figures 3-1 and 3-2 we have plotted corresponding values of I and ΔX thus defined for each of the sixteen years 1954–1969 for each of the eight

---

[a] Capital coefficients require net national product data, and those in turn require depreciation data. Belgium and Switzerland offer depreciation data only from 1956; Sweden offers none at all.

33

34

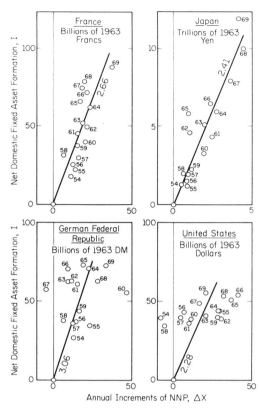

Figure 3-1. Capital coefficients in France, Japan, Germany, and the United States.

countries. If for any country from any of the sixteen points a straight line were drawn to the origin, the slope of that line would represent the value of the capital coefficient for that year in that country. To avoid cluttering the diagrams, such lines have not been drawn explicitly.

For each country one straight line through the origin has been drawn, however. For each country, sum net investment over the sixteen years and call the result $\sum I$. Sum incremental net national product over the same sixteen years and call the result $\sum \Delta X$. The slope of the straight line through the origin shows the ratio

$$\frac{\sum I}{\sum \Delta X} = b$$

representing the overall capital coefficient for the entire period 1954–1969.

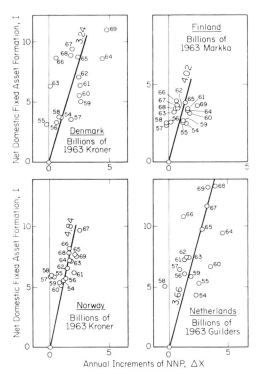

Figure 3-2. Capital coefficients in Denmark, Finland, Norway, and the Netherlands.

The eight values of b appear as labels on the straight lines through the origins in Figures 3-1 and 3-2 as well as in the first column of Table 3-1.

Table 3-1. Capital Coefficients, Propensities to Save, Calculated and Actual Growth Rates in Eight Countries 1953–1969

	b	$1 - c$	Calculated $g_X \equiv (1 - c)/b$	Actual g_X where $e^{16g}X \equiv X(1969)/X(1953)$
Denmark	3.24	0.131	0.040	0.040
Finland	4.02	0.177	0.044	0.046
France	2.66	0.138	0.052	0.053
Germany*	3.06	0.167	0.055	0.059
Japan	2.41	0.223	0.093	0.091
Netherlands	3.66	0.171	0.047	0.048
Norway	4.84	0.192	0.040	0.039
United States	2.28	0.081	0.035	0.034

*Federal Republic.

Two questions are raised by Figures 3-1 and 3-2. First, in each country could the sixteen implicit, undrawn, lines through the origin be said to cluster around the drawn one? The answer is that even the poor clustering in our Figures 3-1 and 3-2 has degrees. Clustering is most pronounced in France and Japan and least pronounced in the United States.[b] How come?

Let investment be motivated by the need for capacity to keep up with demand—as the Harrod-Domar model assumed it to be. Still, investment is always to some extent postponable. But it is less postponable under rapid growth than under slow growth: Demand is catching up more rapidly, and the issue of expanding capacity is pressing with more urgency. Furthermore, investment is less likely to be postponed under smooth growth than under stop-and-go growth. With demand growing smoothly there is less uncertainty about the exact time at which demand has outgrown capacity for good. With demand growing smoothly, the responsiveness of the capital market to a new stock issue or the attractiveness of credit terms will both fluctuate less than under stop-and-go growth. Postponement of investment, then, is less likely to bring a more responsive capital market or more attractive credit terms.

All this leads to the conclusion that investment would be more closely geared to incremental net national product in rapidly and smoothly growing economies like France and Japan, than it would be in a jerkily and slowly growing economy like the United States. Figure 3-1 and 3-2 show that such was actually the case.

The second question raised by Figures 3-1 and 3-2 is whether or not the eight countries differ in their capital coefficients. They do: The highest value 4.84 (Norway) is about $2\frac{1}{8}$ times the lowest value 2.28 (United States). The national ranking of our capital coefficients is roughly the same as that of Leibenstein's [6] U.N. data for 1949–1959—with the United States as the big exception.

National differences in capital coefficients are not surprising: From Bergström [1], 289, Grosse [4], 220–221, Leibenstein [6], 27, Lindberger [7], 45–52, and Lundberg [9], 110–111, we know that capital coefficients differ markedly among industries. Hence national capital coefficients must reflect national industry mix. And the smaller a country is, the more one-sided its industry mix is likely to be. Thus the traditionally high Norwegian capital

---

[b] The German cluster is much better than it looks: Adding in 1960 the Saar and West Berlin to the territory covered means, in effect, treating the 1960 Saar and West Berlin product as an increment to the German product *without* treating existing Saar and West Berlin capital stock as German investment. Since that existing capital stock is not known, we made no attempt to remedy the anomaly. As a result, the slope of a straight line connecting the 1960 point with the origin must be too low.

coefficient must reflect the high capital coefficients of electric power generation [4], [7], and transoceanic transportation [4]. The high Finnish capital coefficient must reflect the high capital coefficient of wood pulp [1], [9].

3. Propensities to Save

What the propensity to save $1 - c$ may be used for in the Harrod-Domar model is the derivation from its Eqs. (9) and (10) of the investment-savings equation

$$(21) \qquad\qquad I = (1 - c)X$$

Part Three, Table 10, lines 6 through 9 of the OECD accounts [10] use the terminology that gross addition to national wealth equals gross fixed asset formation *plus* change in stocks *minus* residual error *plus* net lending to the rest of the world. A Harrod-Domar economy is a closed one, so there is no lending to or borrowing from the rest of the world, and Eq. (10) of the Harrod-Domar model rules out change in stocks. Ignoring the residual error, then, Harrod-Domar gross saving equals gross addition to national wealth equals gross fixed asset formation. Harrod-Domar net saving at 1963 prices equals I as defined in Section 2 above. Harrod-Domar net national product at 1963 prices equals X as defined there.

In Figures 3-3 and 3-4 we have plotted corresponding values of I and X thus defined for each of the sixteen years 1954–1969 for each of the eight countries. If for any country for any of the sixteen points a straight line were drawn to the origin, the slope of that line would represent the value of the propensity to save for that year in that country. The sixteen lines would cluster very heavily. To avoid the congestion, they have not been drawn explicitly.

For each country one straight line through the origin has been drawn. For each country, sum net investment over the sixteen years as before and call the result $\sum I$. Sum net national product over the same sixteen years and call the result $\sum X$. The slope of the straight line through the origin shows the ratio

$$\frac{\sum I}{\sum X} = 1 - c$$

representing the overall propensity to save for the entire period 1954–1969.

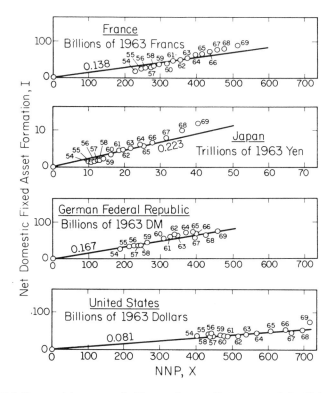

Figure 3-3. Propensities to save in France, Japan, Germany, and the United States.

The eight values of $1 - c$ appear as labels on the straight lines through the origins in Figures 3-3 and 3-4 as well as in the second column of Table 3-1.

Figures 3-3 and 3-4 raise the same two questions as did Figures 3-1 and 3-2. In each country could the sixteen implicit, undrawn, lines through the origin be said to cluster around the drawn one? The answer is that the cluster is far better than it was in Figures 3-1 and 3-2. Furthermore, no noticeable difference between the marginal and the average propensity to save exists in Finland, Germany, Norway, or the United States. But in Denmark, France, Japan, and the Netherlands the marginal propensity to save is visibly higher than the average one. This is another way of saying that the Danish, French, Japanese, and Dutch average propensity to save must have been rising from 1954 to 1969.

The second question raised by Figures 3-3 and 3-4 is whether or not the eight countries differ in their propensities to save. They do indeed: The

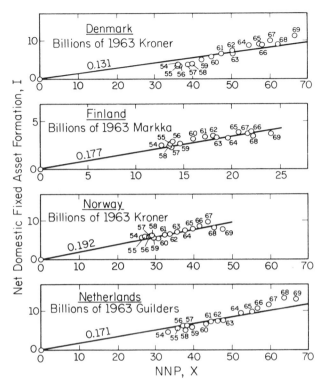

Figure 3-4. Propensities to save in Denmark, Finland, Norway, and the Netherlands.

highest value 0.223 (Japan) is about $2\frac{3}{4}$ times the lowest value 0.081 (United States).[c] How can such differences be explained? Much of them will be

---

[c] The United States capital coefficient and propensity to save are both understated, because United States government expenditure on machinery and equipment is treated as government current expenditure rather than as gross domestic fixed asset formation. How much understated?

Government gross fixed asset formation, defined as excluding machinery and equipment, is known, [10], Part Three, Table 7, Line 19. Deduct it from gross domestic fixed asset formation *minus* machinery and equipment, [10], Part Three, Table 1, Lines 3 *minus* 3c, and find nongovernment gross fixed asset formation other than machinery and equipment. Domestic is around $\frac{4}{3}$ of nongovernment gross fixed asset formation other than machinery and equipment. Suppose the fraction $\frac{4}{3}$ applied to machinery and equipment as well. Then gross domestic fixed asset formation *with* government expenditure on machinery and equipment included would be around $\frac{1}{6}$ higher than as recorded without. If the same were true of net domestic fixed asset formation, then our understated capital coefficient and propensity to save should both be raised by $\frac{1}{6}$ to 2.66 and 0.095, respectively. Even so, still no other country would have lower values than the United States.

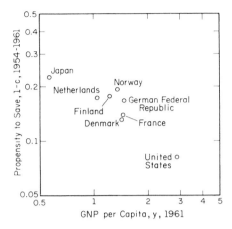

Figure 3-5. Propensity to save as a function of gross national product per capita, international cross section.

explained by per capita gross national product. Use Part One, lower table p. 10 to define

$y \equiv$ gross national product at market prices per capita in U.S. dollars for 1961

In Figure 3-5 we have plotted corresponding values of $1 - c$ and y for each of the eight countries. On the double-logarithmic scale used, the relationship is well approximated by a negatively sloped straight line.

Why negatively sloped? Remember that we have measured saving by measuring investment. OECD accounts know only investment in physical capital. If, as they advance, economies invest more in human capital (education) and less in physical capital, the propensity to save as measured will drop as observed.

4. Calculated Versus Actual Growth Rates

The solution (11) of the Harrod-Domar model finds the proportionate rate of growth of output to equal the ratio between the propensity to save and the capital coefficient. That ratio is shown in the third column of Table 3-1 and may be confronted with the actual rate of growth shown in the fourth column. Should we congratulate ourselves on the good correspondence between calculated and actual growth rate?

Much of the correspondence must be inherent: Let growth be steady-state growth and let v and t be any two points of time. That a variable X is growing at the steady-state rate g_X may then be defined

(22) $$X(t) \equiv e^{g_X(t-v)}X(v)$$

Now we estimated the overall propensity to save $1 - c$ as $\sum I/\sum X$ and the overall capital coefficient b as $\sum I/\sum \Delta X$, hence

$$\frac{1-c}{b} \equiv \frac{\sum \Delta X}{\sum X} \equiv \frac{X(1969) - X(1953)}{X(1954) + \cdots + X(1969)}$$

With $v \equiv 1953$ and $t \equiv 1954, \ldots, 1969$ use (22) upon this:

(23) $$\frac{1-c}{b} \equiv \frac{e^{16g_X} - 1}{e^{g_X} + \cdots + e^{16g_X}}$$

In the denominator, find the sum of the terms of the geometrical progression and write

$$\frac{1-c}{b} \equiv 1 - e^{-g_X}$$

So far in this section, all equalities have been definitional ones. But

$$e^x = 1 + x + \frac{x^2}{2!} + \frac{x^3}{3!} + \cdots$$

Replacing x by $-g_X$ we have

(24) $$1 - e^{-g_X} \simeq g_X$$

where the symbol $\simeq$ is used to denote approximate equality. In addition to this approximation, the steady-state growth assumed in (22) was an approximation to actual growth, hence the sum of the terms of the geometrical progression in the denominator of (23) was also an approximation. Approximations (22) as well as (24) being good, we expect the third column of Table 1 to be a good approximation to the fourth column.

Notes

[1] Bergström, V., "Industriell utveckling, industrins kapitalbildning och finanspolitiken," *Svensk finanspolitik i teori och praktik* (Erik Lundberg, ed.), Stockholm, 1971.

[2] Cassel, G., *Theoretische Sozialökonomie*, Leipzig, 1923, 51–52; *The Theory of Social Economy*, New York, 1924, 62–63.

[3] Domar, E. D., "Capital Expansion, Rate of Growth, and Employment," *Econometrica*, Apr. 1946, **14,** 137–147.

[4] Grosse, R. N., "The Structure of Capital," *Studies in the Structure of the American Economy* (W. Leontief, ed.), New York, 1953.

[5] Harrod, R. F., *Towards a Dynamic Economics*, London, 1948.

[6] Leibenstein, H., "Incremental Capital-Output Ratios and Growth Rates in the Short Run," *Rev. Econ. Stat.*, Feb. 1966, **48,** 20–27.

[7] Lindberger, L., *Investeringsverksamhet och sparande*, Stockholm, 1956.

[8] Lundberg, E., *Studies in the Theory of Economic Expansion*, London, 1937.

[9] Lundberg, E., *Produktivitet och räntabilitet*, Stockholm, 1961.

[10] *National Accounts of O.E.C.D. Countries/Comptes nationaux des pays de l'O.C.D.E. 1953–1969*, Paris, 1971.

4 Von Neumann Steady-State Growth

Several years before the appearance of the Harrod-Domar model, von Neumann [1], [2] had built a superior growth model with explicit optimization in it: His solution weeds out all but the most profitable process or processes. His solution also tells us which goods will be free and which economic. Like Cassel and Harrod-Domar, von Neumann ignores technological progress.

1. Notation

Variables

$C \equiv$ aggregate cost
$g \equiv$ proportionate rate of growth
$K \equiv$ money capital advanced by capitalists
$P \equiv$ price
$R \equiv$ aggregate revenue
$r \equiv$ rate of interest
$X \equiv$ level of a process

Parameters

$a_{ij} \equiv$ input of ith good per unit of jth process level
$s_{ij} \equiv$ output of ith good per unit of jth process level

2. Processes, Their Level, and Their Rate of Growth

A von Neumann process may have several inputs and several outputs, and its unit level may arbitrarily be defined as the unit of any one input or any one output per unit of time.

43

Let there be m goods and n processes. Operated at unit level, the jth process converts $a_{1j}, \ldots, a_{mj}$ units of the m goods absorbed as inputs into $s_{1j}, \ldots,$ s_{mj} units of the m goods supplied as output. The coefficients a_{ij} and s_{ij} are nonnegative technological parameters. The level of the jth process is the pure number X_j by which unit level should be multiplied in order to get actual input or output. The proportionate rate of growth g_j of the level of the jth process is defined

(1) $$X_j(t + 1) \equiv [1 + g_j(t)]X_j(t)$$

Does the von Neumann model have substitution in it? It does. First, there is substitution in production, for although each process has parametric input coefficients a_{ij} and output coefficients s_{ij}, the same good may occur as an output in more than one process, hence may be produced in more than one way. Second, there is substitution in consumption, for labor is a good like any other, hence is reproducible: Labor is simply the output of one or more processes whose inputs are consumers' goods. Although each such process has parametric input coefficients a_{ij} and output coefficients s_{ij}, labor may occur as an output in more than one process, hence may be produced in more than one way—by being fed, so to speak, alternative menus.

Does the von Neumann model have capital in it? It does; in fact it incorporates the time element of production in a particularly ingenious way. In the von Neumann model all processes have a period of production of one time unit, but this is less restrictive than it sounds: As for circulating capital, if consumable wine has a period of production of two years, simply define two distinct processes and goods as follows. The first process absorbs zero-year old wine and supplies one-year old wine; the second absorbs one-year old wine and supplies two-year old wine. As for fixed capital, if the useful life of machines is two years, again define two distinct processes and goods. The first process absorbs zero-year old machines and supplies one-year old machines; the second absorbs one-year old machines and supplies two-year old machines!

Since a process absorbing its input at time t supplies its output at time $t + 1$, should the time coordinate of its level be that of its input or that of its output? Arbitrarily let it be the latter.

3. Excess Demand Must Be Nonpositive

Let the level of the jth process be $X_j(t + 1)$. As a result, the input of the ith good required at time t is $a_{ij}X_j(t + 1)$. Because the coefficient a_{ij} is a parameter, the input of the ith good in the jth process $a_{ij}X_j(t + 1)$ is growing at the same proportionate rate $g_j(t + 1)$ as the level $X_j(t + 1)$ of that process.

Let the level of the jth process be $X_j(t)$. As a result, the output of the ith good supplied at time t is $s_{ij}X_j(t)$. Because the coefficient s_{ij} is a parameter, the output of the ith good in the jth process $s_{ij}X_j(t)$ is growing at the same proportionate rate $g_j(t)$ as the level $X_j(t)$ of that process.

Use (1) and write excess demand for the ith good in the jth process at time t as

$$a_{ij}X_j(t + 1) - s_{ij}X_j(t) = \{a_{ij}[1 + g_j(t)] - s_{ij}\}X_j(t)$$

which will be positive, zero, or negative as the brace of the right-hand side is positive, zero, or negative. Now some processes may have positive, some zero, and some negative excess demand for the ith good. But feasibility requires overall excess demand to be nonpositive: The sum of all inputs of the ith good required in all processes must be smaller than or equal to the sum of all outputs of it supplied in all processes:

$$(2) \quad a_{i1}X_1(t + 1) + \cdots + a_{in}X_n(t + 1) \le s_{i1}X_1(t) + \cdots + s_{in}X_n(t)$$

where $i = 1, \ldots, m$. If for the ith good the less-than sign applies, that good at time t is a free good having a zero price: $P_i(t) = 0$. Rule out the uninteresting case that all goods are free and assume that at least one is not, i.e., that in the system (2) at least one equality sign applies.

4. Profits Must Be Nonpositive

At time $t + 1$ let the jth process be operated at unit level. The inputs required at time t at unit level are a_{ij}, $i = 1, \ldots, m$. Such inputs are purchased at the prices $P_i(t)$, $i = 1, \ldots, m$. Hence the input costs at unit level are $a_{ij}P_i(t)$, and their sum is $a_{1j}P_1(t) + \cdots + a_{mj}P_m(t)$. The outputs supplied at time $t + 1$ at unit level are s_{ij}, $i = 1, \ldots, m$. Such outputs are sold at prices $P_i(t + 1)$, $i = 1, \ldots, m$. Hence the revenues at unit level are $s_{ij}P_i(t + 1)$, and their sum is $s_{1j}P_1(t + 1) + \cdots + s_{mj}P_m(t + 1)$.

Now under pure competition and freedom of entry, profits must be nonpositive, hence for the jth process the sum of all input cost at time t with interest added at the rate r must be greater than or equal to the sum of all revenue at time $t + 1$:

$$(3) \quad [1 + r(t)][a_{1j}P_1(t) + \cdots + a_{mj}P_m(t)]$$

$$\ge s_{1j}P_1(t + 1) + \cdots + s_{mj}P_m(t + 1)$$

where $j = 1, \ldots, n$. If for the jth process the greater-than sign applies, that process at time $t + 1$ is a money-losing one to be operated at zero level: $X_j(t + 1) = 0$. Rule out the uninteresting case that all processes are money-losing ones and assume that at least one is not, i.e., that in the system (3) at least one equality sign applies.

5. Equilibrium

Von Neumann thought of equilibrium growth as steady-state balanced growth of all process levels. Balanced growth of process levels means that the proportionate rates of growth of all process levels are identical:

(4) $$g_1(t) = \cdots = g_n(t)$$

Steady-state growth of process levels means that the proportionate rates of growth of all process levels are stationary:

(5) $$g_j(t + 1) = g_j(t); \qquad j = 1, \ldots, n$$

Von Neumann also required the rate of interest and all prices to be stationary:

(6) $$r(t + 1) = r(t)$$

(7) $$P_i(t + 1) = P_i(t); \qquad i = 1, \ldots, m$$

6. Growth Patterns of Goods

In Inequality (2) use (1) to express all $X_j(t + 1)$ in terms of $X_j(t)$. Use (4) to strip $g_j(t)$ of all its subscripts and (5) to strip it of its time coordinate:

(2a) $$(1 + g)[a_{i1}X_1(t) + \cdots + a_{in}X_n(t)] \le s_{i1}X_1(t) + \cdots + s_{in}X_n(t)$$

where $i = 1, \ldots, m$. The system (2a) expresses the growth pattern of goods: If the less-than sign of (2a) applies, the economy more than reproduces what it absorbed one period earlier of the ith good raised by the growth rate g, hence the ith good is growing at a rate higher than g. If the equality sign of (2a) applies, the ith good is growing at the rate g. Now we have assumed that at least one equality sign applies, hence the equilibrium rate of growth g must be the rate of growth of the slowest-growing good or goods. Goods growing faster than that become free. Notice that while process-level growth is balanced, goods growth is unbalanced!

7. Profitability Patterns of Processes

In Inequality (3), use (6) and (7) to strip $r(t)$ and $P_i(t)$ of their time co-ordinates:

(3a) $$(1 + r)(a_{1j}P_1 + \cdots + a_{mj}P_m) \geq s_{1j}P_1 + \cdots + s_{mj}P_m$$

where $j = 1, \ldots, n$. The system (3a) expresses the profitability pattern of processes: If the greater-than sign of (3a) applies, revenue from the process falls short of its cost one period earlier with interest added to it at the rate r, hence the process has an internal rate of return less than r. If the equality sign of (3a) applies, the process has an internal rate of return equalling r. Now we have assumed that at least one equality sign applies, hence the equilibrium rate of interest must be the internal rate of return of the most profitable process or processes. Processes less profitable than that will remain unused.

8. Rate of Growth Equals Rate of Interest

Take another look at Inequality (2a), valid for the ith good. Multiply by the price P_i of that good:

(2b) $$(1 + g)[a_{i1}P_iX_1(t) + \cdots + a_{in}P_iX_n(t)]$$
$$\leq s_{i1}P_iX_1(t) + \cdots + s_{in}P_iX_n(t)$$

There are m such inequalities, one for each good. But recall that if for the ith good the less-than sign applies, the ith good is free, i.e., $P_i = 0$. Hence multiplying by P_i has the effect of killing all less-than signs. Now define aggregate cost paid out at time $t - 1$ and aggregate revenue received at time t, respectively:

(8) $$C(t - 1) \equiv \sum_{i=1}^{m} \sum_{j=1}^{n} [a_{ij}P_iX_j(t)]$$

(9) $$R(t) \equiv \sum_{i=1}^{m} \sum_{j=1}^{n} [s_{ij}P_iX_j(t)]$$

Then add the m inequalities (2b) with the less-than signs killed:

(2c) $$(1 + g)C(t - 1) = R(t)$$

Now take another look at Inequality (3a) valid for the jth process. Multiply it by the level of that process at time t, $X_j(t)$:

(3b) $(1 + r)[a_{1j}P_1 X_j(t) + \cdots + a_{mj}P_m X_j(t)]$

$$\geq s_{1j}P_1 X_j(t) + \cdots + s_{mj}P_m X_j(t)$$

There are n such inequalities, one for each process. But recall that if for the jth process the greater-than sign applies, the jth process is a money-losing one, i.e., $X_j(t) = 0$. Hence multiplying by $X_j(t)$ has the effect of killing all greater-than signs. Use the definitions (8) and (9) and add the n inequalities (3b) with the greater-than signs killed:

(3c) $$(1 + r)C(t - 1) = R(t)$$

Take (2c) and (3c) together and conclude:

(10) $$g = r$$

9. Conclusion

If an equilibrium exists, the rate of growth of all process levels equals the rate of interest. The equilibrium rate of growth of all process levels equals the rate of growth of the slowest-growing good or goods. Goods growing faster than that become free. The equilibrium rate of interest equals the internal rate of return of the most profitable process or processes. Processes less profitable than that remain unused.

Using nonelementary mathematics, von Neumann proved that such an equilibrium does exist.

10. The Capitalists

The von Neumann model may have real live capitalists in it, lending money capital to the process operators to carry them over their one-year period of production. At time $t - 1$ let the capitalists lend the process operators the sum of money

(11) $$K(t - 1) = C(t - 1)$$

Now the economy is a closed one, so what the process operators as a whole are purchasing, the process operators as a whole are selling:

(12) $$C(t - 1) = R(t - 1)$$

The capitalists will charge interest at the rate r, so at time t the sum of money owed to them is

$$(13) \qquad K(t) = (1 + r)C(t - 1)$$

But process operators have been prudent and have used nothing but the most profitable process or processes, hence at constant prices the value of their output at time t will have grown to $R(t)$ as defined by (3c). Take (3c) and (13) together and see that $K(t) = R(t)$. Consequently, at time t process operators can pay their debt to the capitalists, provided of course that the sale of their output at constant prices can be financed. It can if the capitalists lend the process operators the sum

$$(11) \qquad K(t) = C(t)$$

Again, what the process operators as a whole are purchasing, the process operators as a whole are selling:

$$(12) \qquad C(t) = R(t)$$

In this way we may continue. New debt forever pays off old debt with interest, and the aggregate debt is a rising one, rising at the rate of growth $g = r$. What makes it all possible is the willingness of the capitalists to save their entire interest earnings.

Thus only labor consumes in the von Neumann model. The entrepreneurs don't consume anything, because their income as entrepreneurs is zero—pure competition and freedom of entry see to that. Capitalists do have an income, but their propensity to consume it is zero.

Notes

[1] Dorfman, R., P. A. Samuelson, and R. Solow, *Linear Programming and Economic Analysis*, New York, 1958, 381–388.

[2] von Neumann, J., "Über ein ökonomisches Gleichungssystem und eine Verallgemeinerung des Brouwerschen Fixpunktsatzes," *Ergebnisse eines mathematischen Kolloquiums*, 8, Leipzig and Vienna, 1937, 73–83, translated as "A Model of General Economic Equilibrium," *Rev. Econ. Stud*, 1945–46, **13,** 1–9.

III. Capital
Deepening

5 Neoclassical Steady-State Growth

Like the Harrod-Domar model, the neoclassical growth model [36], [38] is an aggregative one: Again entrepreneurs produce a single good from labor and an immortal capital stock of that good, hence investment is the act of setting aside part of output for installation as capital stock. Capital stock is the result of accumulated savings under an autonomously given propensity to save, and available labor force is growing autonomously.

But unlike the Harrod-Domar model, the neoclassical model permits substitution between labor and capital. The result is twofold: First, there can be full employment; second, income distribution may now be explained.

Unfortunately economists possess no simple model of collective bargaining, so we shall assume the money—but not the real—wage rate to be growing autonomously. If this is not quite neoclassical [36], [38], it is at least realistic.

Section I of this chapter defines variables and parameters. Section II specifies the model mathematically. Section III finds solutions for the proportionate rates of growth. Section IV finds solutions for the levels of variables. Section V applies the model to four special cases.

An appendix summarizes empirical measurements of parameters and variables.

I. Notation

Variables

$C \equiv$ consumption
$g_v \equiv$ proportionate rate of growth of the variable v where $v \equiv C, I, \kappa, L, P,$ $S, X,$ and Y
$g_{gv} \equiv$ proportionate rate of acceleration of the variable v where $v \equiv S$
$I \equiv$ investment
$\imath \equiv$ internal rate of return
$k \equiv$ present gross worth of a physical unit of capital stock
$\kappa \equiv$ physical marginal productivity of capital stock
$L \equiv$ labor employed
$n \equiv$ present net worth of a physical unit of capital stock

53

$P \equiv$ price of good
$r \equiv$ rate of interest
$S \equiv$ physical capital stock
$W \equiv$ wage bill
$X \equiv$ physical output
$Y \equiv$ national money income
$Z \equiv$ profits bill

Parameters

$\alpha, \beta \equiv$ exponents of production function
  $c \equiv$ propensity to consume
  $F \equiv$ available labor force
  $g_p \equiv$ proportionate rate of growth of parameter p where $p \equiv F$, M, and w
  $M \equiv$ multiplicative factor of production function
  $v \equiv$ propensity to save $1 - c$
  $w \equiv$ money wage rate

All flow variables refer to the instantaneous rate of that variable measured on a per annum basis. The parameters listed are stationary except F, M, and w, whose proportionate rates of growth are stationary. Symbols t and τ are time coordinates. The symbol e is Euler's number, the base of natural logarithms.

II. The Equations of the Model

Eight variable growth rates are listed in Section I. To all apply the definition

(1) through (8)
$$g_v \equiv \frac{dv}{dt}\frac{1}{v}$$

Define investment as the derivative of capital stock with respect to time

(9)
$$I \equiv \frac{dS}{dt}$$

Let the entrepreneurs apply the Cobb-Douglas[a] production function

(10)
$$X = ML^\alpha S^\beta$$

---

[a] First written (but without the multiplicative factor) by Wicksell [42], 128.

where $0 < \alpha < 1$; $0 < \beta < 1$; $\alpha + \beta = 1$; and $M > 0$. Let profit maximization under pure competition equalize real wage rate and physical marginal productivity of labor:

$$(11) \qquad \frac{w}{P} = \frac{\partial X}{\partial L} = \alpha \frac{X}{L}$$

Physical marginal productivity of capital is

$$(12) \qquad \kappa \equiv \frac{\partial X}{\partial S} = \beta \frac{X}{S}$$

Multiply (12) by price of output P to find value marginal productivity of capital. Define money profits earned on each physical unit of capital stock S as its value marginal productivity. Then multiply by S to find money profits earned on capital stock S

$$(13) \qquad Z \equiv \kappa PS = \beta PX$$

Under full employment, available labor force must equal labor employed:

$$(14) \qquad F = L$$

Define the wage bill as the money wage rate *times* employment:

$$(15) \qquad W \equiv wL$$

Define national money income as the sum of the wage bill and the profits bill:

$$(16) \qquad Y \equiv W + Z$$

Let consumption be a fixed proportion of output:

$$(17) \qquad C = cX$$

where $0 < c < 1$. Output equilibrium requires output to equal the sum of consumption and investment demand for it, or inventory would either accumulate or be depleted:

$$(18) \qquad X = C + I$$

III. Solutions for Proportionate Rates of Growth

Define, as Hahn and Matthews [18] did, steady-state growth as stationary proportionate rates of growth. Our system (1) through (18) may then be said to possess a set of steady-state solutions for its equilibrium proportionate rates of growth. To find that set, let us begin by inserting (14) into (10) and differentiate the latter with respect to time:

$$(19) \qquad g_X = g_M + \alpha g_F + \beta g_S$$

From (17), (18), and (1) through (9) find

$$(20) \qquad g_S = \frac{(1 - c)X}{S}$$

Differentiate (20) with respect to time, use (1) through (8), and (19), and find the proportionate rate of acceleration

$$(21) \qquad g_{gS} \equiv \frac{dg_S}{dt} \frac{1}{g_S} = \alpha \left(\frac{g_M}{\alpha} + g_F - g_S \right)$$

In (21) there are only three possibilities: If $g_S > g_M/\alpha + g_F$, then $g_{gS} < 0$. If

$$(22) \qquad g_S = \frac{g_M}{\alpha} + g_F$$

then $g_{gS} = 0$. Finally, if $g_S < g_M/\alpha + g_F$, then $g_{gS} > 0$. Consequently, if greater than (22) g_S is falling; if equal to (22) g_S is stationary; and if less than (22) g_S is rising. Furthermore, g_S cannot alternate around (22), for differential equations trace continuous time paths, and as soon as the g_S-path crossed (22) it would have to stay there. Finally, g_S cannot converge toward anything else than (22), for if it did, by letting enough time elapse we could make the left-hand side of (21) less than any arbitrarily assignable positive constant ε, however small, without the same being possible for the right-hand side. Our steady-state test, then, shows that g_S either equals $g_M/\alpha + g_F$ from the outset or, if it doesn't, will converge toward that value.

Insert (22) into (19) and find

$$(23) \qquad g_X = \frac{g_M}{\alpha} + g_F$$

Then guess the rest:

$$(24) \qquad g_C = g_X$$

$$(25) \qquad g_I = g_X$$

$$(26) \qquad g_\kappa = 0$$

$$(27) \qquad g_L = g_F$$

$$(28) \qquad g_P = g_w - \frac{g_M}{\alpha}$$

$$(29) \qquad g_Y = g_F + g_w$$

To convince himself that those are indeed solutions, the reader should take derivatives with respect to time of (9) through (12), (16) with (13) through (15) inserted into it, (17), and (18). He should then use the definitions (1) through (8), insert the solutions (22) through (29), and convince himself that each equation is satisfied.

IV. Solutions for Levels

So much for proportionate rates of growth. Let us now turn to the allocation of resources. Admittedly there isn't much scope for resource allocation in our one-good economy. To allow for the full allocation of resources we would at least have to assume each of two goods to serve interchangeably as a consumers' or as a producers' good—as we shall do in Chapter 8.

Our present one-good economy does, however, have one resource-allocation problem: Entrepreneurs produce a single good from labor and an immortal capital stock of that good, hence investment is the act of setting aside part of output for installation as capital stock. How large a part? The parameter governing this choice is the propensity to save $v \equiv 1 - c$. Oddly enough, v occurs nowhere in the solutions (22) through (29) for the proportionate rates of growth. We suspect, then, that there is more to growth theory than the solutions for proportionate rates of growth! There is not only a resource-allocation problem, but also an inherent price mechanism for solving it. To see all that, we shall have to solve for levels of variables.

1. *Solving for Revenue PX*

Insert (14) into (11) and find revenue

$$(30) \qquad PX = \frac{wF}{\alpha}$$

If we could now find a solution for physical output X, we could divide it into our revenue solution PX and find price P.

2. Solving for Physical Output X

Let us begin by finding the investment-output ratio. Insert (17) into (18) and find

$$(31) \qquad \frac{I}{X} = v \equiv 1 - c$$

Now according to the production function (10), output X is a function of capital stock S rather than of investment I. But according to (1) through (9):

$$(32) \qquad S \equiv \frac{I}{g_S}$$

where our steady-state growth, as specified by (22), permits us to express g_S solely in terms of parameters. Inserting (31) into (32) we find

$$(33) \qquad S = \frac{Xv}{g_S}$$

Inserting (14) and (33) into the production function (10) we find our solution for physical output

$$(34) \qquad X = M^{1/\alpha} \left(\frac{v}{g_S}\right)^{\beta/\alpha} F$$

Here the propensity to save v occurs for the first time: The elasticity of physical output with respect to the propensity to save is β/α. The reader may convince himself that (34) is indeed growing at the rate (23) said it should be.

3. Solving for the Capital Coefficient S/X

Write (33) as

$$(33) \qquad \frac{S}{X} = \frac{v}{g_S}$$

Here the propensity to save v occurs for the second time: The elasticity of the capital coefficient with respect to the propensity to save is unity! Under steady-state growth, as specified by (22), the capital coefficient (33) is stationary, just as it was in the Harrod-Domar model. But the neoclassical and the Harrod-Domar models display stationary capital coefficients for very different reasons. In the Harrod-Domar model the capital coefficient was *assumed* to be stationary; in the neoclassical model it is *found* to be.

4. *Solving for Capital Intensity S/L*

Insert (34) into (33), divide by (14), and find

$$(35) \qquad \frac{S}{L} = \left(\frac{Mv}{g_S}\right)^{1/\alpha}$$

Here the propensity to save v occurs for the third time: The elasticity of capital intensity with respect to the propensity to save is $1/\alpha$. Since M is rising, capital intensity is rising. This phenomenon has been called "capital deepening."

5. *Solving for Price P*

Divide our revenue solution (30) by our physical output solution (34) and find the solution for price

$$(36) \qquad P = \left[M \left(\frac{v}{g_S}\right)^{\beta} \right]^{-1/\alpha} \frac{w}{\alpha}$$

Here the propensity to save v occurs for the fourth time: The elasticity of price with respect to the propensity to save is $-\beta/\alpha$. In other words, price is lower, the higher the propensity to save. Again the reader may convince himself that (36) is indeed growing at the rate (28) said it should be.

6. *Solving for the Real Wage Rate w/P*

Write (36) as

$$(36) \qquad \frac{w}{P} = \alpha \left[M \left(\frac{v}{g_S}\right)^{\beta} \right]^{1/\alpha}$$

Here the propensity to save v occurs for the fifth time: The elasticity of the real wage rate with respect to the propensity to save is β/α. The real wage rate, then, is higher, the higher the propensity to save, and a Wicksell Effect is present: "The capitalist saver is thus, fundamentally, the friend of labour ..." [42], 164.

Wicksell continued: "... though the technical inventor is not infrequently its enemy." In the neoclassical model is he? Under a production function like (10) with neutral and disembodied technological progress, is the technical inventor hostile or friendly? Notice that he affects the real wage

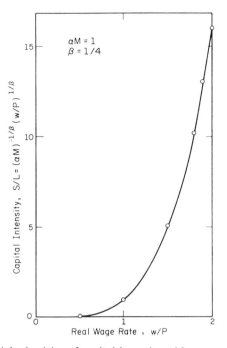

Figure 5-1. The high elasticity of capital intensity with respect to real wage rate.

rate as expressed by (36) in two entirely different ways: First it is due to the technical inventor, and him alone, that the real wage rate is rising over time. Were it not for the growing factor M in (36), the latter would remain stationary. To that extent the technical inventor is friendly. But, second, the level of the real wage rate as expressed by (36) has g_S raised to the power $-\beta/\alpha$ in it. And according to (22) $g_S = g_M/\alpha + g_F$, hence the higher g_M, the lower the level (36). To that extent the technical inventor is hostile.

7. A Price Mechanism

Let us pause for a moment to see the price mechanism inherent in the neoclassical growth model. In our one-good economy the price of labor is the money wage rate w, and the price of a physical unit of capital stock is P, hence the relative price of labor is w/P or simply the real wage rate.

A rising real wage rate should induce factor substitution in the form of rising capital intensity, called "capital deepening" in this book. That it will do just that is readily apparent if we take (35) and (36) together and find how a profit-maximizing entrepreneur's desired capital intensity responds to the real wage rate facing him:

$$(37) \qquad \frac{S}{L} = (\alpha M)^{-1/\beta} \left(\frac{w}{P}\right)^{1/\beta}$$

The elasticity of desired capital intensity with respect to the real wage rate is, then, $1/\beta$. The high elasticity for relastic values of β is apparent from Figure 5-1, drawn for $\alpha M = 1$ and $\beta = 1/4$.

But if desired capital intensity is so elastic with respect to the real wage rate, how come our capital-intensity solution (35) and our real-wage-rate solution (36) show exactly the same time trend, due solely to their common factor $M^{1/\alpha}$? Shouldn't every one per cent increase in the real wage rate be accompanied by a four per cent increase in capital intensity?

It should for a given value of M for which Figure 5-1 was drawn. But over time, M is growing, and (37) shows the elasticity of capital intensity with respect to M to be $-1/\beta$ which is negative. So there is no contradiction between our static Figure 5-1 and our dynamic solutions (35) and (36).

8. Physical Capital Stock S; Physical Marginal Productivity κ; Internal Rate of Return ι; Rate of interest r; and Inflation

With (34) inserted into it, (33) will be a solution for physical capital stock S. With (33) inserted into it, (12) will be a solution for the physical marginal productivity of capital:

$$(38) \qquad \kappa = \frac{\beta g_S}{v}$$

Here the propensity to save v occurs for the sixth time: The elasticity of physical marginal productivity with respect to the propensity to save is *minus* One!

Nothing but stationary parameters appears on the right-hand side of (38). Since capital stock is immortal, a physical unit of capital stock added at time τ will, then, have the physical marginal productivity (38) at any time from $t = \tau$ to $t = \infty$.

What sort of value marginal productivity will it have? Let it be perfectly foreseen by the entrepreneurs that price is growing at the proportionate rate g_P:

$$(39) \qquad P(t) = P(\tau)e^{g_P(t-\tau)}$$

But let the entrepreneurs in the neoclassical growth model be purely competitive ones, hence price is beyond their control. At time t, value marginal productivity is, then

$$(40) \qquad \frac{\partial[P(t)X(t)]}{\partial S(t)} = P(t)\kappa$$

As seen from time τ, value marginal productivity at time t is $P(t)\kappa e^{-r(t-\tau)}$ where e is Euler's number, the base of natural logarithms, and r is the discount rate applied by the entrepreneurs. Define present gross worth of the physical unit of capital stock as the present worth of all its future value marginal productivities:

$$(41) \qquad k(\tau) \equiv \int_\tau^\infty P(t)\kappa e^{-r(t-\tau)}\, dt$$

Let the rate of inflation be less than the discount rate:

$$(42) \qquad g_P < r$$

Then insert (39) into (41) and carry out the integration. Since in the resulting expression all variables refer to the same time τ, we may purge it of τ:

$$(43) \qquad k = \frac{P\kappa}{r - g_P}$$

Define the present net worth of the physical unit of capital stock as gross worth *minus* price:

$$n \equiv \left(\frac{\kappa}{r - g_P} - 1 \right) P$$

Define the internal rate of return ι as that value of r which makes net worth equal to zero, hence

$$(44) \qquad \iota \equiv \kappa + g_P$$

where κ stands for (38) and g_P for (28). In English: The internal rate of return ι of the physical unit of capital stock added at time τ equals the physical marginal productivity (38) of that unit at any time from $t = \tau$ to $t = \infty$ *plus* the proportionate rate of inflation (28).

Now we assumed that $0 < c < 1$, hence households save. Let there be a money capital market in which firms may borrow by selling claims upon themselves, and savers may lend by buying those claims. The rate of interest is the yield on such claims. Now if

$$(45) \hspace{4cm} r = \iota$$

where ι is defined by (44), then the present net worth of the physical unit of capital stock added at time τ will be zero; that unit will be the last one the entrepreneurs will wish to add at that time; our full-employment assumption (14) will be validated; and all our growth solutions (22) through (29) will apply. But who secures the equality between the rate of interest r and the internal rate of return ι as defined by (44)?

The equality may have to be secured by a monetary authority maintaining and expanding a stock of claims: As long as $r = \iota$, physical assets are growing in accordance with (22), physical output in accordance with (23), and the price of either in accordance with (28), hence the value of assets as well as transactions is displaying steady-state growth. If there is any assets or transactions demand for money at all, then, such demand must be growing. As long as $r = \iota$, the monetary authority cannot satisfy the demand in any way other than by expanding its stock of claims, and with it the money supply.

Does money matter, then? Let the monetary authority be expanding its stock of claims more rapidly than described, lowering the rate of interest r and making $r < \iota$ as defined by (44). Consequently, the present net worth of of the physical unit of capital stock added at time τ will now be positive, and that unit will no longer be the last one the entrepreneurs will wish to add at that time: They will wish to add *more* than that. But at continued full employment physical output can grow no more rapidly than at our equilibrium rate (23). In the scramble for goods, the price of goods will be rising more rapidly than at our equilibrium rate (28)—thus violating (28). In conclusion, then, money does matter: If the monetary authority depresses the rate of interest below its equilibrium value (45), extra inflation will be generated, over and above the equilibrium rate of inflation (28).

Instead, let the monetary authority be expanding its stock of claims less rapidly than described above, raising the rate of interest r and making $r > \iota$ as defined by (44). Then the present net worth of the physical unit of capital stock added at time τ will be negative. Again that unit will not be the last one the entrepreneurs will wish to add at that time: Now they will wish to add *less* than that. This will reduce the demand for goods, and inventory of goods will be accumulating as long as the physical output were growing at our equilibrium rate (23). Eventually, then, physical output will be growing less rapidly than at our equilibrium rate (23)—thus violating (23) as well as our full-employment assumption (14). Again money matters: If the monetary authority raises the rate of interest above its equilibrium value (45), unemployment will be generated—as it was in the United States in 1970. Might such unemployment not modify money-wage-rate demands and thus slow down inflation? It might or might not. At the present state of our knowledge of the money-wage-rate formation mechanism, honesty would seem to dictate treating g_w as a parameter—as we are doing throughout this book.

9. *Income Distribution W and Z*

With (14) inserted, (15) will be a solution for the wage bill:

(46) $$W = wF$$

With (30) inserted into it, (13) will be a solution for the profits bill

(47) $$Z = \frac{wF\beta}{\alpha}$$

Insert (46) and (47) into (16), use (30), and find

(48) $$Y = \frac{wF}{\alpha} = PX$$

(49) $$\frac{W}{Y} = \alpha$$

(50) $$\frac{Z}{Y} = \beta$$

The distributive shares are, then, the exponents of the Cobb-Douglas production function (10). The propensity to save v is absent from (48) through (50).

10. *Consumption and the Golden Rule of Accumulation*

Investment was the act of setting aside part of output for installation as capital stock. How large a part constituted the one resource-allocation problem in our one-good economy. Is there an optimal solution to that problem? Suppose a social objective were to maximize the level of consumption at a particular time [33]. Insert (34) into (17), take the derivative with respect to the propensity to consume c, and set that derivative equal to zero:

$$\frac{\partial C}{\partial c} = \left(1 - \frac{\beta}{\alpha}\frac{c}{1-c}\right) X = 0$$

Setting the parenthesis equal to zero gives us the Golden Rule of Accumulation

(51) $$c = \alpha$$

Thus the level of consumption at a particular time would be maximized by a propensity to consume equalling the elasticity of output with respect to labor input!

Would it have made any difference if instead the social objective had been to maximize the level of consumption *per capita* at a particular time [41]? Since F is a parameter we have

$$\frac{\partial(C/F)}{\partial c} = \left(1 - \frac{\beta}{\alpha}\frac{c}{1-c}\right)\frac{X}{F} = 0$$

which again gives us (51). Consequently it makes no difference whether the social objective is maximization of consumption or of consumption *per capita*. An implication of such maximization is found by writing (51) as $1 - c \equiv v = \beta$, and inserting into (38):

(52) $$g_S = \kappa$$

reminiscent of the result (10) in Chapter 4 on the von Neumann growth model. Thus maximizing consumption or consumption *per capita* implies that the proportionate rate of growth of capital stock (and output) equals the physical marginal productivity of capital. As we shall see in our Appendix, accumulation in the United States has been quite far from observing the Golden Rule of Accumulation.

11. *Properties of Solutions*

We have now solved for the levels of variables. Our solutions (31) for the investment-output ratio, (33) for the capital coefficient, (38) for the physical marginal productivity of capital, (44) for the internal rate of return, and (49), (50) for the distributive shares were found to be stationary. All other solutions for levels are nonstationary, because they contain one or more of our three nonstationary parameters, i.e., available labor force F, the multiplicative factor M, and the money wage rate w. All solutions are obviously real. Under the assumptions made about domains of the parameters, all solutions are positive.

12. *Conclusions*

Our solutions for levels have brought out two things. First, although the propensity to save v occurs nowhere in the solutions (22) through (29) for the proportionate rates of growth, it does play a role in the determination of levels: Physical output, the capital coefficient, capital intensity, price, the real wage rate, and the physical marginal productivity of capital are all affected by it.

Second, our solutions for levels brought out explicitly the price mechanism at work in the neoclassical growth model. The labor-capital price ratio was w/P or the real wage rate. A rising real wage rate induced enough capital deepening for full-employment investment to absorb full-employment saving at all times in an economy whose capital is growing more rapidly than its labor.[b]

V. Four Special Cases

Let us illuminate the generality of the neoclassical growth model by applying it to four special cases. In each case leaving all other parameters as specified in the master model, develop, first, the zero-population-growth case by setting $g_F = 0$; second the Böhm-Bawerk-Wicksellian case of pure capital deepening by setting $g_F = g_M = 0$; third the case of extreme underdevelopment by setting $c = 1$; and fourth the Ricardian case of stationary nature as a factor of production. The first three cases are collapses. The fourth case is an extension: Incorporate nature as a third factor of production along with labor and capital stock, but let the production function remain linearly homogeneous.

---

[b] Such reliance on a price mechanism could only expect a hostile reaction by Keynesians. Eisner [12] claimed that the real trouble with capitalism was a floor under the interest rate and that the Harrod-Domar capital coefficient was variable anyway. But if the Harrod-Domar solution for the proportionate rate of growth of output as the ratio between the propensity to save and the capital coefficient, is to be a solution at all, it can contain nothing but parameters on its right-hand side, Harrod's and Eisner's verbal afterthoughts notwithstanding. Domar understood this when he said "we shall make the heroic assumption that [the ratio between incremental capacity and investment] is constant" [10], 74.

Going back to Eqs. (19) through (21), in each case let us find out what is happening to (1) capital stock, (2) output, (3) physical marginal productivity of capital and (4) the real wage rate.

1. *Zero Population Growth*

Insert $g_F = 0$ into (19) and find

(19a) $$g_X = g_M + \beta g_S$$

Initially, then, if $g_S > g_M/\alpha$ then $g_X < g_S$: Output will be growing less rapidly than does capital stock. How is the latter growing? For $g_F = 0$, (21) collapses into

(21a) $$g_{gS} = g_M - \alpha g_S$$

Again, there are three possibilities: If $g_S > g_M/\alpha$, then $g_{gS} < 0$. If

(22a) $$g_S = \frac{g_M}{\alpha}$$

then $g_{gS} = 0$. Finally, if $g_S < g_M/\alpha$, then $g_{gS} > 0$. Consequently, since g_S cannot converge toward anything else than (22a), it will do just that. According to (19a) g_X will then converge toward g_M/α.

What is happening to the physical marginal productivity of capital? Take the derivative of (12) with respect to time, insert (1) through (8), and find

(12a) $$g_\kappa = g_X - g_S$$

Insert (19a) into (12a) and find

(53) $$g_\kappa = g_M - \alpha g_S$$

Comparing (53) to (21a) we find that the rate of growth of physical marginal productivity equals the rate of acceleration of capital stock. Since the latter converges to zero, so must the former.

What is happening to the real wage rate? Take the derivative of (11) with respect to time, insert (1) through (8) and (14), and find

(11a) $$g_w - g_P = g_X - g_F$$

Insert $g_F = 0$ and (19a) into (11a) and find

(54) $$g_w - g_P = g_M + \beta g_S$$

But we have just seen that g_S will converge to (22a). Consequently, according to (54) $g_w - g_P$ will converge to g_M/α. So it would under positive population growth, cf. our solution (28). Is labor better off at all under zero population growth, then? It is indeed, for the level of the real wage rate as expressed by (36) has g_S raised to the power $-\beta/\alpha$ in it. According to (22) $g_S = g_M/\alpha + g_F$, hence the higher g_F, the lower the level (36)!

In conclusion, the zero-population-growth economy is growing by accumulating capital and by enjoying technological progress. The proportionate rates of growth of output, capital stock, and the real wage rate will all converge to the same value, i.e., g_M/α. The proportionate rate of growth of the physical marginal productivity of capital will converge to zero.

2. The Böhm-Bawerk-Wicksellian Case

Insert $g_F = g_M = 0$ into (19) and find

$$(19b) \qquad\qquad g_X = \beta g_S$$

Initially, then, if $g_S > 0$ then $g_X < g_S$: Output will be growing less rapidly than does capital stock. How is the latter growing? For $g_F = g_M = 0$, (21) collapses into

$$(21b) \qquad\qquad g_{g_S} = -\alpha g_S$$

Again there are three possibilities: If $g_S > 0$ then $g_{g_S} < 0$. If

$$(22b) \qquad\qquad g_S = 0$$

then $g_{g_S} = 0$. Finally, if $g_S < 0$ then $g_{g_S} > 0$. Consequently, since g_S cannot converge toward anything else than (22b), it will do just that. According to (19b) g_X will then converge toward zero.

But as long as there is still positive saving—and we are upholding the assumption that $0 < c < 1$—how could capital stock stop growing? The answer is it couldn't. The *absolute* rate of growth of capital stock $I \equiv dS/dt = (1 - c)X$ is not vanishing. But the *proportionate* rate of growth of capital stock $g_S = (1 - c)X/S$ is vanishing, because according to (19b) output X is growing less rapidly than does capital stock S.

What is happening to the physical marginal productivity of capital? Insert (19b) into (12a) and find

$$(55) \qquad\qquad g_\kappa = -\alpha g_S$$

Comparing (55) to (21b) we find that the rate of growth of physical marginal productivity equals the rate of acceleration of capital stock. Since the latter converges to zero, so must the former.

But the physical marginal productivity of capital itself also converges to zero: Since (1) through (18) still hold, (33) and (38) still hold, and the latter converges to zero, because g_S does.[c]

What is happening to the real wage rate? Insert $g_F = 0$ and (19b) into (11a) and find

$$(56) \qquad\qquad g_w - g_P = \beta g_S$$

But we have just seen that g_S will converge to (22b). Consequently, according to (56) $g_w - g_P$ will converge to zero.

In conclusion, the Böhm-Bawerk-Wicksellian economy is growing solely by accumulating capital. Unlike the zero-population-growth case, the Böhm-Bawerk-Wicksellian case will converge to a stationary economy: The proportionate rates of growth of output, capital stock, physical marginal productivity, and the real wage rate will all converge to zero! The economy is being saturated with capital accumulation in the sense that the physical marginal productivity of capital itself will converge to zero.

3. Extreme Underdevelopment

Insert $c = 1$ into (20) and find

$$(20c) \qquad\qquad g_S = 0$$

Hence according to (19):

$$(19c) \qquad\qquad g_X = g_M + \alpha g_F$$

What is happening to physical marginal productivity of capital? Insert (19c) and (20c) into (12a) and find

$$(57) \qquad\qquad g_\kappa = g_M + \alpha g_F$$

The proportionate rates of growth of output (19c) and of physical marginal productivity of capital (57), then, are the same.

What is happening to the real wage rate? Insert (19c) into (11a) and find

$$(58) \qquad\qquad g_w - g_P = g_M - \beta g_F$$

---

[c] This is as close as this author could ever come to Schumpeter's notion of a zero rate of interest in a stationary economy!

so there is a race between technological and population growth: If $g_M > \beta g_F$ the real wage rate will be growing; if $g_M = \beta g_F$ the real wage rate will remain stationary; and if $g_M < \beta g_F$ the real wage rate will be decaying.

In conclusion, the extremely underdeveloped economy has no capital accumulation but is growing by technological and population growth. The proportionate rates of growth of output and the physical marginal productivity of capital are positive and the same. Unlike the zero-population-growth case and the Böhm-Bawerk-Wicksellian case, then, the extremely underdeveloped economy has an ever-rising physical marginal productivity of capital! This in itself is politically explosive. Even worse, there is a very real possibility that the extremely underdeveloped economy may have a decaying real wage rate.

Such a thing could not happen in a highly developed economy with plenty of capital accumulation, or could it? Let us now turn Ricardian and see that it could.

4. The Ricardian Case

Let us turn Ricardian (and very modern) by emphasizing the boundary imposed upon man by irreproducible nature, called "land" by Ricardo.

Call nature N and let it be a third factor of production along with labor and capital stock in the production function, but let the latter remain linearly homogeneous:

$$(10a) \qquad X = ML^\alpha S^\beta N^\gamma$$

where $0 < \alpha < 1$; $0 < \beta < 1$; $0 < \gamma < 1$; $\alpha + \beta + \gamma = 1$; $M > 0$; and N is stationary. Because N is stationary, insertion of (14) and differentiation of (10a) with respect to time will still give us

$$(19) \qquad g_X = g_M + \alpha g_F + \beta g_S$$

From (17), (18), and (1) through (9) find as before that

$$(20) \qquad g_S = \frac{(1 - c)X}{S}$$

Differentiate (20) with respect to time, use (1) through (8), write $\beta - 1 = -(\alpha + \gamma)$, and find the proportionate rate of acceleration

$$(21d) \qquad g_{gS} \equiv \frac{dg_S}{dt}\frac{1}{g_S} = (\alpha + \gamma)\left(\frac{g_M + \alpha g_F}{\alpha + \gamma} - g_S\right)$$

In (21d) there are only three possibilities: If $g_S > (g_M + \alpha g_F)/(\alpha + \gamma)$, then $g_{gS} < 0$. If

(22d)
$$g_S = \frac{g_M + \alpha g_F}{\alpha + \gamma}$$

then $g_{gS} = 0$. Finally, if $g_S < (g_M + \alpha g_F)/(\alpha + \gamma)$, then $g_{gS} > 0$. Consequently, since g_S cannot converge toward anything else than (22d), it will do just that. Insert (22d) into (19) and find

(23d)
$$g_X = \frac{g_M + \alpha g_F}{\alpha + \gamma}$$

So output and capital stock will eventually be growing at the same steady-state proportionate rate (22d) and (23d). That rate may be lower than when nature was ignored, but it is still a steady-state rate!

What is happening to the physical marginal productivity of capital? Take the derivative of (12) with respect to time, insert (1) through (8), and find

(12a)
$$g_\kappa = g_X - g_S$$

Insert (19) into (12a) and find

(59)
$$g_\kappa = (\alpha + \gamma) \left(\frac{g_M + \alpha g_F}{\alpha + \gamma} - g_S \right)$$

Comparing (59) to (21d) we find that the rate of growth of physical marginal productivity equals the rate of acceleration of capital stock. Since the latter converges to zero, so must the former.

What is happening to the real wage rate? Take the derivative of (11) with respect to time, insert (1) through (8) and (14) and find

(11a)
$$g_w - g_P = g_X - g_F$$

Insert (19) into (11a) and find

(60)
$$g_w - g_P = g_M - (1 - \alpha)g_F + \beta g_S$$

But we have just seen that g_S will converge to (22d). Insert (22d) into (60), write $1 - \alpha = \beta + \gamma$, and find the growth rate of the real wage rate converging to

(61)
$$g_w - g_P = \frac{g_M - \gamma g_F}{\alpha + \gamma}$$

So if the natural-resource elasticity of output γ is high enough, if labor-force growth g_F is high enough, or if technological progress g_M is low enough, even a highly developed economy with plenty of capital accumulation can generate a decaying real wage rate.

VI. Empirical Orders of Magnitude

Our appendix summarizes empirical measurements of some parameters and variables used in the neoclassical growth model.

Appendix: Empirical Measurements

1. The Production Function

Denison [8] and Barger [3] used a straightforward Cobb-Douglas production function with α and β equalling 0.70 and 0.30, respectively, but with labor force decomposed as follows:

$$(59) \qquad F = NHE$$

where N = number of men; H = hours worked per man; and E = an education factor. It follows from (59) that $g_F = g_N + g_H + g_E$. Table 5-1 reproduces the Barger measurements for all terms of our Eq. (19) thus expanded for four advanced economies in the period 1950–1964.

Table 5-1. Sources of Growth in Four Countries, 1950–1964 [3]

Proportionate Rate of Change per annum of	German Federal Republic	Sweden	U.K.	U.S.
Output, g_X	0.0652	0.0384	0.0276	0.0332
Multiplicative Factor, g_M	0.0351	0.0169	0.0122	0.0144
Number of Men, g_N	0.0127	0.0070	0.0061	0.0119
Hours Worked per Man, g_H	−0.0051	−0.0019	−0.0024	−0.0027
Education, g_E	0.0022	0.0039	0.0053	0.0073
Adjusted Labor, g_F	0.0098	0.0090	0.0090	0.0165
Capital Stock, g_S	0.0774	0.0505	0.0304	0.0241
$\alpha g_F + \beta g_S$	0.0301	0.0215	0.0154	0.0188

In our production function (10) two crucial assumptions were made about α and β: First, they were assumed to sum to One. Second, they were assumed to remain stationary.

Do α and β sum to One? Empirical measurements marked by an asterisk in our Table 5-2 simply assume the distributive shares to represent α and β, hence do not help answer the question. But Douglas [11], Niitamo [30], and Aukrust [2] found α and β to sum to very close to One. Walters [40], on the other hand, fitted a Cobb-Douglas function to Solow's [37] data and found

73

Table 5-2. Empirical Estimates of Cobb-Douglas Production Functions

Country	Period	Labor Exponent α	Capital Exponent β	Rate of Growth of M g_M	
U.S.	1899–1922	0.81	0.23	—	[11]
		0.78	0.15	—	
		0.73	0.25	—	
Finland	1925–1952	0.74	0.26	0.012	[30]
Norway	1900–1955	0.76	0.20	0.018	[2]
U.S.	1909–1928⎫			⎧0.012	[37]
	1929–1948⎬	—	0.35*	⎨0.019	
	1909–1948⎭			⎩0.015	
U.S.	1900–1953	0.84*	—	0.011	[25]
U.S.	1919–1949	1.08	0.19	0.012	[40]
U.S.	1929–1947⎫			⎧0.019	[31]
	1947–1960⎬	0.75*	—	⎨0.025	
	1929–1960⎭			⎩0.021	
Norway	1900–1956	0.91	0.28	0.014	[35]
Sweden,	1952–1960⎫			⎧0.018	[5]
Mfg.	1960–1968⎬	0.52*	—	⎨0.030	
	1952–1968⎭			⎩0.026	

*Factor's share of national income.

clearly increasing returns to scale: Walter's $\alpha + \beta = 1.27$. Ringstad [35], 126, did the same for Norway and found $\alpha + \beta = 1.19$.

Are α and β stationary? All empirical measurements listed in our Table 5-2 assume them to be, hence do not help answer the question. But Brown and Popkin [6] distinguished three periods in the history of the United States nonfarm product:

Period	$\alpha + \beta$
1890–1918	1.47
1919–1937	1.04
1938–1958	1.04

To Norwegian net national product data 1900–1956 Ringstad [35], 128–131, fitted an ingenious nonhomogeneous production function having the same substitution properties as the corresponding Cobb-Douglas function but having a *variable* scale elasticity. The average scale elasticity for the entire period 1900–1956 found by using such a variable-elasticity-of-scale function was 1.24, not very different from the sum $\alpha + \beta = 1.19$ found by fitting the corresponding Cobb-Douglas function. But Ringstad's more sophisticated method paid off in finding a marked *decline* of scale elasticity

Table 5-3. Empirical Estimates of Constant-Elasticity-of-Substitution Production Functions

Country	Period	Elasticity of Substitution, σ	Rate of Growth of Overall Factor Productivity*	
U.S.	1909–1949	0.57	0.018	[1]
U.S.	1919–1960	0.58	0.021	[23]
U.S.	1899–1960	0.32	0.019	[7]

*[1] and [23] used a Hicks-neutral CES function, hence in those two cases the rate of growth of overall factor productivity equals the rate of growth g_γ of the multiplicative factor γ in Eq. (60).

over the period—not inconsistent with the cruder findings by Brown and Popkin.

During the 1960's the Cobb-Douglas form was losing ground to the constant-elasticity-of-substitution form[d] of the production function. The linearly-homogeneous, Hicks-neutral-technological-progress version [1], 230, of it is

$$(60) \qquad X = \gamma[(1 - \delta)L^{-\rho} + \delta S^{-\rho}]^{-1/\rho}$$

where L, S, and X have the same meanings as in our Cobb-Douglas function; where γ is an efficiency parameter whose growth measures Hicks-neutral technological progress; where δ is a distribution parameter; and where $\rho > -1$ is a substitution parameter. The elasticity of substitution $\sigma \equiv 1/(1 + \rho)$.

Using the form (60),[e] Arrow, Chenery, Minhas, and Solow [1], 244, and Kendrick and Sato [23], 985, found elasticities of substitution equalling 0.57 and 0.58, respectively. Using a form allowing for Hicks-nonneutral technological progress, Jungenfelt [21] found a very similar value for Sweden, i.e., 0.57 for manufacturing and transportation and 0.59 for agriculture; whereas David and van de Klundert [7], 360, found the even lower value 0.32, "a value that casts very serious doubt on the appropriateness of the (unitary elasticity of substitution) Cobb-Douglas form ... ". Perhaps labor and capital are poorer substitutes than Cobb-Douglas functions assume them to be. Still, in his survey of production functions, Walters [39], 38, concludes

---

[d] First written (but without the multiplicative factor) by Solow [36], 77.

[e] Kendrick-Sato used exactly, not merely "basically," the same form, for their $a \equiv \delta$; $b \equiv 1 - \delta$; $T \equiv \gamma$; and $\theta \equiv \rho$.

that "... the simple Cobb-Douglas function should not be confidently rejected at this stage."

Does it matter whether or not labor and capital are poorer substitutes than Cobb-Douglas functions assume them to be? In theory it does: "If the elasticity of substitution is small it is 'difficult' to get increased output by increasing just one factor, since diminishing returns set in strongly and rapidly," [32], 326. Historically we have not increased just one factor, but we have increased capital far more than labor. Assuming the elasticity of output with respect to labor to be initially 0.7 and the elasticity of substitution to be 0.5, Nelson [32], 327, found the resulting drag on growth to be very small: "the drag of a less than unitary elasticity of substitution should have reduced the annual growth rate of output by less than 0.001 percentage points a year below that which a Cobb-Douglas model would have predicted." In their survey of technical progress [24], 25, Kennedy and Thirlwall agreed: "To affect substantially ... the measure of technical progress, σ would have to be markedly different from unity, and the difference between the rates of growth of capital and labour unrealistically wide." Whether or not labor and capital are poorer substitutes than Cobb-Douglas functions assume them to be, then, seems to matter more in theory than in practice. And certainly Table 5-3 shows that the rates of technological progress generated by constant-elasticity-of-substitution functions are not very different from those generated by Cobb-Douglas functions.

For the United States 1909–1960, Japan 1930–1960, and the German Federal Republic 1850–1959 (using the very long time series calculated by Hoffman [19]), Beckmann and Sato [4] offered nine alternative linear or log-linear specifications of technological progress. They estimated the values of the coefficients and wrote out the form of the implied production functions. The overall conclusion drawn from this very comprehensive work was that "the estimated values of the coefficients in these [production] functions tend to make the approximation to Cobb-Douglas usually quite close. This is yet another confirmation of the robustness of the Cobb-Douglas function for empirical work." [4], 93.

Perhaps an *aggregate* production function is an illusion. Dhrymes [9] examined two-digit-industry data for the United States in 1957 and found elasticities of substitution to vary from 0.19 to 1.98. Seven of the 17 industries had elasticities higher than One. Dhrymes concluded: "the constant elasticity of substitution function does not describe uniformly well the productive process of the industries considered." Specifically, "consumer-oriented industries tend to be characterized by higher elasticities of substitution than do investment-oriented industries." Examining [15] more generally the existence of aggregate production functions, Fisher concluded [16] that they "are not generally even good approximate descriptions of the technical production possibilities of a diverse economy." To a disaggregated model we turn in Chapter 8.

Perhaps disembodied technological progress is also an illusion. Much technological progress makes its way into the economy in the form of new and physically different hardware rather than in the form of modified existing hardware. How much? To United States data for 1929–1958 Intriligator [20] fitted a homogeneous Cobb-Douglas function allowing for disembodied progress, progress embodied in capital, and progress embodied in labor. Disembodied and embodied technological progress were found to be 0.017 and 0.04 per annum, respectively. Capital-embodied progress was found to be more important than labor-embodied progress. But using the unusually comprehensive Australian annual census data, Lydall [29] examined 54 industries over the decade 1949/50–1959/60 and found disembodied technological progress to have been of greater importance. To embodied technological progress we turn in Chapters 9 and 10.

2. The Propensity to Save

Has the propensity to save remained stationary? For a time it was believed to, but for the United States 1869–88 to 1950–59 Kuznets [28], 248–249 found the following net savings proportions of net product:

1869–1888	0.13
1889–1908	0.14
1909–1928	0.12
1929–1938	0.03
1946–1955	0.10
1950–1959	0.10

Over the same period, the United Kingdom propensity to save was also found to be declining, but for Australia, Canada, Denmark, Italy, Japan, and Norway Kuznets found rising propensities to save. Using Kuznets data, Klein [25] found the propensity to consume to have been rising by $\frac{1}{8}$ of one per cent semiannually in the United States 1900–1953. Kendrick and Sato [23], 981, found the propensity to save to have declined by 0.006 per annum in the United States 1919–1960.

From such production-function and consumption-function data it is apparent that the Golden Rule of Accumulation has not been observed: For the United States the elasticity of output with respect to capital stock, β, has been at least twice as high as the propensity to save, $1 - c$!

3. The Proportionate Rate of Growth of Output

Turning now to the realism of our solutions of the neoclassical growth model, we ask if the proportionate rate of growth of output has indeed remained stationary—as our solution (22) tells us it should have. For the United States net national product Kuznets [27], 23, found the following proportionate rates of growth:

1869/78–1884/93	0.054
1884/93–1909/18	0.035
1914/23–1934/43	0.020
1939/48–1948/57	0.043

Interpreting Kendrick [22] data, Fellner [14] judged United States growth 1884–1957 to have been almost steady-state.

4. The Capital Coefficient

Has the capital coefficient remained stationary—as our solution (33) tells us it should have? Kravis [26] found the ratio between United States tangible reproducible assets and national income to have been decaying by an average proportionate rate of 0.0075 per annum 1900/1909–1949/1957. Fabricant [13] found the decay to be picking up speed: From an average proportionate rate of decay of 0.005 per annum 1889–1919 to 0.013 per annum 1919–1957. Klein [25] found an average proportionate rate of decay of one-third of one per cent semiannually 1900–1953. Swedish decay seemed slower: Bergström [5], 292, found an average proportionate rate of decay of 0.001 per annum in Swedish manufacturing industry 1952–1968. The trendlessness of the capital coefficient, then, is not borne out by the data.

5. Capital Intensity

Has capital intensity been growing—as our solution (35) tells us it should have? For the United States Kravis [26] did find tangible reproducible assets, in 1929 prices, per man hour to have grown by an average proportionate rate of 0.015 per annum 1900/1909–1949/1957. Swedish capital-intensity growth seemed faster: Bergström [5], 292, found an average proportionate rate of growth of 0.049 per annum in Swedish manufacturing industry 1952–1968.

6. The Real Wage Rate

Has the real wage rate been growing—as our solution (36) tells us it should have? For the United States Kravis [26] did find the wage rate in 1929 prices per man hour to have grown by an average proportionate rate of 0.025 per annum 1900/1909–1949/1957. Kendrick and Sato [23], 977, found an average proportionate rate of growth of 0.026 per annum 1919–1960.

Well and good, but have the real wage rate and capital intensity been growing at the *same* proportionate rate—as a comparison between our solutions (35) and (36) shows they should have? Not quite! Apparently the real wage rate has been growing at a rate $1\frac{2}{3}$ times higher than that of capital intensity.

7. The Physical Marginal Productivity of Capital

Has the physical marginal productivity of capital remained stationary—as our solution (38) tells us it should have? Kravis [26] estimated for the United States what he called the "price" of capital, defined in our own notation as $(\beta Y/Y)(PX/PS) \equiv \kappa$, and found it to be:

1900–1909	0.088
1910–1919	0.095
1920–1929	0.087
1930–1939	0.056
1939–1948	0.092
1949–1957	0.089

Kendrick and Sato [23], 980, found no pronounced trend either. For Britain, Phelps Brown and Weber [34] found that over each span 1870–1913 and 1924–1938 the ratio between yield and replacement cost of capital remained almost stationary.

8. The Distributive Shares

Have the distributive shares remained stationary—as our solutions (49) and (50) tell us they should have? For the United States Klein [25] found labor's share to be the only one of his Great Ratios which was trendless. Grant [17] found that labor's share "underwent little change between 1899 and 1929." Kuznets [28], 173, found the proportionate share of income from assets to have remained stationary from the turn of the century to the end of World War II. After that, the share declined—as it did in Belgium, Norway, Japan, Australia, and New Zealand. Kravis [26] questioned the constancy of the shares in the United States. Kendrick and Sato [23], 980, found labor's share to have increased 1919–1960 from 0.72 to 0.78 or by 0.002 per annum. For Britain, Phelps Brown and Weber [34] found that over each span 1870–1913 and 1924–1938 wage and salary earnings remained much the same proportion of national income. For Sweden, Jungenfelt [21] found labor's share fluctuating inversely with the business cycle around a stationary value of slightly above 0.70.

Notes

[1] Arrow, K. J., H. B. Chenery, B. S. Minhas, and R. M. Solow, "Capital-Labor Substitution and Economic Efficiency," *Rev. Econ. Stat.*, Aug. 1961, **43**, 225–250.

[2] Aukrust, O., "Investment and Economic Growth," *Prod. Meas. Rev.*, Feb. 1959, **16**, 35–53.

[3] Barger, H., "Growth in Developed Nations," *Rev. Econ. Stat.*, May 1969, **51**, 143–148.

[4] Beckmann, M. J., and R. Sato, "Aggregate Production Functions and Types of Technical Progress: A Statistical Analysis," *Am. Econ. Rev.*, Mar. 1969, **59**, 88–101.

[5] Bergström, V., "Industriell utveckling, industrins kapitalbildning och finanspolitiken," *Svensk finanspolitik i teori och praktik* (Erik Lundberg ed.), Stockholm, 1971.

[6] Brown, M., and J. Popkin, "A Measure of Technological Change and Returns to Scale," *Rev. Econ. Stat.*, Nov. 1962, **44**, 402–411.

[7] David, P. A., and T. van de Klundert, "Biased Efficiency Growth and Capital-Labor Substitution in the U.S., 1899–1960," *Am. Econ. Rev.*, June 1965, **55**, 357–390.

[8] Denison, E. F., *Why Growth Rates Differ*, Washington, D.C., 1967.

[9] Dhrymes, P. J., "Some Extensions and Tests for the CES Class of Production Functions," *Rev. Econ. Stat.*, Nov. 1965, **47**, 357–366.

[10] Domar, E. D., "Capital Expansion, Rate of Growth, and Employment," as reprinted in *Essays in the Theory of Economic Growth*, New York, 1957.

[11] Douglas, P. H., "Are there Laws of Production?" *Am. Econ. Rev.*, Mar. 1948, **38**, 1–41.

[12] Eisner, R., "On Growth Models and the Neoclassical Resurgence," *Econ. Jour.*, Dec. 1958, **68**, 707–721.

[13] Fabricant, S., *Basic Facts on Productivity Change*, New York, 1958.

[14] Fellner, W., "Measures of Technological Progress in the Light of Recent Growth Theories," *Am. Econ. Rev.*, Dec. 1967, **57**, 1073–1098.

[15] Fisher, F. M., "The Existence of Aggregate Production Functions," *Econometrica*, Oct. 1969, **37**, 553–577.

[16] Fisher, F. M., "Reply," *Econometrica*, Mar. 1971, **39**, 405.

[17] Grant, A., "Issues in Distribution Theory: The Measurement of Labor's Relative Share, 1899–1929," *Rev. Econ. Stat.*, Aug. 1963, **45**, 273–279.

[18] Hahn, F. H., and R. C. O. Matthews, "The Theory of Economic Growth: A Survey," *Econ. Jour.*, Dec. 1964, **74**, 779–902.

[19] Hoffman, W. G., *Das Wachstum der deutschen Wirtschaft seit der Mitte des* 19. *Jahrhunderts*, New York, 1965.

[20] Intriligator, M. D., "Embodied Technical Change and Productivity in the United States 1929–1958," *Rev. Econ. Stat.*, Feb. 1965, **47**, 65–70.

[21] Jungenfelt, K. G., *Löneandelen och den ekonomiska utvecklingen*, Stockholm, 1966.

[22] Kendrick, J. W., *Productivity Trends in the United States*, Princeton 1961.

[23] Kendrick, J. W., and R. Sato, "Factor Prices, Productivity, and Economic Growth," *Am. Econ. Rev.*, Dec. 1963, **53**, 974–1003.

[24] Kennedy, C., and A. P. Thirlwall, "Surveys in Applied Economics: Technical Progress," *Econ. Jour.*, Mar. 1972, **82**, 11–72.

[25] Klein, L. R., and R. F. Kosobud, "Some Econometrics of Growth: Great Ratios of Economics," *Quart. Jour. Econ.*, May 1961, **75**, 173–198.

[26] Kravis, I. B., "Relative Income Shares in Fact and Theory," *Am. Econ. Rev.*, Dec. 1959, **49**, 917–949.

[27] Kuznets, S., "Quantitative Aspects of the Economic Growth of Nations, VI. Long-Term Trends in Capital Formation Proportions," *Econ. Dev. Cult. Change*, July 1961, **9**, 3–124.

[28] Kuznets, S., *Modern Economic Growth, Rate, Structure and Spread*, New Haven and London, 1966.

[29] Lydall, H. F., "Technical Progress in Australian Manufacturing," *Econ. Jour.*, Dec. 1968, **78**, 807–826.

[30] Niitamo, O., "The Development of Productivity in Finnish Industry 1925–1952," *Prod. Meas. Rev.*, Nov. 1958, **15**, 1–12.

[31] Nelson, R. R., "Aggregate Production Functions and Medium-Range Growth Projections," *Am. Econ. Rev.*, Sep. 1964, **54**, 575–606.

[32] Nelson, R. R., "The CES Production Function and Economic Growth Projections," *Rev. Econ. Stat.*, Aug. 1965, **47**, 326–328.

[33] Phelps, E., "The Golden Rule of Accumulation: A Fable for Growthmen," *Am. Econ. Rev.*, Sep. 1961, **51**, 638–643.

[34] Phelps Brown, E. H. and B. Weber, "Accumulation, Productivity, and Distribution in the British Economy, 1870–1938," *Econ. Jour.*, June 1953, **63**, 263–288.

[35] Ringstad, V., "Econometric Analyses Based on a Production Function with Neutrally Variable Scale-Elasticity," *Swed. Jour. Econ.*, June 1967, **69**, 115–133.

[36] Solow, R. M., "A Contribution to the Theory of Economic Growth," *Quart. Jour. Econ.*, Feb. 1956, **70,** 65–94.

[37] Solow, R. M., "Technical Change and the Aggregate Production Function," *Rev. Econ. Stat.*, Aug. 1957, **39,** 312–330.

[38] Tinbergen, J., "Zur Theorie der langfristigen Wirtschaftsentwicklung," *Weltw. Archiv*, May 1942, **55,** 511–549.

[39] Walters, A. A., "Production and Cost Functions: An Econometric Survey," *Econometrica*, Jan.-Apr. 1963, **31,** 1–66.

[40] Walters, A. A., "A Note on Economies of Scale," *Rev. Econ. Stat.*, Nov. 1963, **45,** 425–427.

[41] Von Weizsäcker, C. C., "Das Investitionsoptimum in einer wachsenden Wirtschaft," *Optimales Wachstum und optimale Standortverteilung* (Erich Schneider ed.), Berlin, 1962, 60–76.

[42] Wicksell, K., *Lectures on Political Economy*, *I*, London, 1934.

6

Steady-State Unbalanced International Growth: Trade

A primary purpose of this book is to come to grips with the full allocation of labor, capital, and goods. Expanding the one-good neoclassical growth model of Chapter 5 into the full-fledged allocation model of Chapter 8 is a difficult task, best performed gradually. We shall do it in three steps.

The first step is to borrow a leaf from international-trade theory. Here there are two countries each of which produces one good. International-trade theory has traditionally assumed that neither labor nor capital are free to move internationally. To Ricardo—and forever after—such lack of factor mobility was the first rationale for a separate theory of international trade. To us it is a welcome simplication: We need worry about the allocation of neither labor nor capital between our two countries. We need to worry only about the allocation of the two goods between the two countries, and even this problem we shall simplify by assuming the two goods to be traded internationally only as consumers' goods.[a]

The second rationale for a separate theory of international trade was the existence of different monetary units in different countries. To us this is an unwelcome complication: Another variable is added to our system, i.e., the exchange rate. But fortunately, at the same time, balance-of-payments equalization adds another equation.

Let us build, then, a two-country neoclassical growth model (Figure 6-1) using prices and the exchange rate as variables and admitting consumer preferences, disparity of the rates of technological progress, and disparity of the rates of growth of the labor forces.[b] Again define, as Hahn and Matthews [6] did, steady-state growth as stationary proportionate rates of growth. In addition define, as Solow and Samuelson [10] did, balanced growth as stationary mutual proportions between physical output of all goods.

---

[a] For international direct investment, see Chapter 7.
[b] Bardhan [2] ignored all four items.

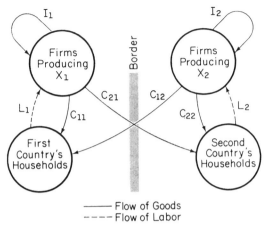

Figure 6-1. Physical flows.

1. Notation

Variables

$C_{hi} \equiv$ consumption in hth country of goods produced in ith country

$E \equiv$ exchange rate in number of monetary units of Country 1 exchanged for one monetary unit of Country 2

$g_v \equiv$ proportionate rate of growth of variable v where $v \equiv C, E, I, L, P, S, X$, and Y

$g_{gv} \equiv$ proportionate rate of acceleration of variable v where $v \equiv S$

$I \equiv$ investment

$L \equiv$ labor employed

$P \equiv$ price of good

$S \equiv$ physical capital stock

$U \equiv$ utility

$X \equiv$ physical output

$Y \equiv$ national money income

Parameters

$A \equiv$ exponent of utility function

$\alpha, \beta \equiv$ exponents of production function

$c \equiv$ propensity to consume

$F \equiv$ available labor force
$g_p \equiv$ proportionate rate of growth of parameter p where $p \equiv F, M,$ and w
$M \equiv$ multiplicative factor of production function
$N \equiv$ multiplicative factor of utility function
$w \equiv$ money wage rate

Subscripts $i = 1, 2$ refer to country number.

All flow variables refer to the instantaneous rate of that variable measured on a per annum basis. The parameters listed are stationary except F, M, and w, whose proportionate rates of growth are stationary. The symbol t is the time coordinate.

2. The Equations of the Model

Eight variable growth rates are listed in Section I. To all apply the definition

(1) through (8)
$$g_{vi} \equiv \frac{dv_i}{dt} \frac{1}{v_i}$$

Define investment as the derivative of capital stock with respect to time

(9)
$$I_i \equiv \frac{dS_i}{dt}$$

Let the entrepreneurs apply the Cobb-Douglas production functions

(10)
$$X_i = M_i L_i^{\alpha_i} S_i^{\beta_i}$$

where $0 < \alpha_i < 1$; $0 < \beta_i < 1$; $\alpha_i + \beta_i = 1$; and $M_i > 0$. Let profit maximization under pure competition equalize real wage rate and physical marginal productivity of labor in each country:

(11)
$$\frac{w_i}{P_i} = \frac{\partial X_i}{\partial L_i} = \alpha_i \frac{X_i}{L_i}$$

Under full employment, available labor force must equal labor employed:

(12)
$$F_i = L_i$$

In this chapter, we shall not explore income distribution, so we define national money incomes simply as the money values of physical outputs:

(13)
$$Y_i \equiv P_i X_i$$

And now for the only allocation problem that arises in our two-country model, i.e., the allocation of consumers' goods between the two countries. That is a straightforward problem of deriving a demand function from a utility function [3], Chapter 2, and we solve it as follows. Within each country let all persons have the same utility function and propensity to consume, but let both differ between countries. Let the utility function of the kth person in the hth country be

$$U_{hk} = N_h C_{h1k}{}^{A_{h1}} C_{h2k}{}^{A_{h2}}$$

where $0 < A_{hi} < 1$ and $N_h > 0$. In the hth country let there be s_h persons, and let the kth person's money income be Y_{hk} where

$$\sum_{k=1}^{s_h} Y_{hk} = Y_h$$

Let all persons in the hth country spend the fraction c_h where $0 < c_h < 1$, of their money income. Then the budget constraint of the kth person in the two countries is

$$c_1 Y_{1k} = P_1 C_{11k} + E P_2 C_{12k}$$

$$c_2 Y_{2k} = \frac{P_1 C_{21k}}{E} + P_2 C_{22k}$$

Maximize the kth person's utility subject to his budget constraint to find his two demand functions. For each country, add the s_h individual demand functions for each good to arrive at its two Graham-type[c] [4] demand functions

(14)
$$C_{11} = \frac{\pi_{11} Y_1}{P_1}$$

(15)
$$C_{12} = \frac{\pi_{12} Y_1}{E P_2}$$

(16)
$$C_{21} = \frac{\pi_{21} E Y_2}{P_1}$$

---

[c] Graham demand functions have income and price elasticities of 1 and −1, respectively. Empirical elasticities of United States import with respect to income were estimated at 0.91 and 1.6 [1]; 1.00 [5]; 1.51 [7]; and 1.27 [8]. Elasticities of United States import with respect to price were estimated at −0.51 and −1 [1]; −0.95 [5]; −0.54 [7]; and −1.1 [8]. Income and price elasticities of the import of 14 other major countries were estimated at 1.37 and −0.90, respectively [7]. Perhaps Graham demand functions are, after all, not entirely "trivial for empirical applications" [9]?

$$(17) \qquad C_{22} = \frac{\pi_{22} Y_2}{P_2}$$

where C_{hi} is the consumption in the hth country of goods produced in the ith country, and where

$$\pi_{hi} \equiv \frac{c_h A_{hi}}{A_{h1} + A_{h2}}$$

National output equilibrium requires output to equal the sum of consumption, export, and investment demand for it:

$$(18) \qquad X_i = \sum_{h=1}^{2} C_{hi} + I_i$$

Balance-of-payments equilibrium requires Country 1's consumption of Country 2's goods to equal Country 2's consumption of Country 1's goods, both being measured in the same monetary unit, or exchange reserves of the ith country would either accumulate or be depleted. Thus

$$(19) \qquad EP_2 C_{12} = P_1 C_{21}$$

3. Solutions for Proportionate Rates of Growth

Insert (12) into (10) and differentiate with respect to time:

$$(20) \qquad g_{Xi} = g_{Mi} + \alpha_i g_{Fi} + \beta_i g_{Si}$$

Use (1) through (9), (18), (19), (14) through (17), and (13) in that order and find

$$g_{Si} = \frac{(1 - c_i) X_i}{S_i}$$

Differentiate (21) with respect to time, use (1) through (8) and (20), and find the proportionate rate of acceleration

$$(22) \qquad g_{gSi} \equiv \frac{dg_{Si}}{dt} \frac{1}{g_{Si}} = \alpha_i \left(\frac{g_{Mi}}{\alpha_i} + g_{Fi} - g_{Si} \right)$$

In (22) there are only three possibilities: If $g_{Si} > g_{Mi}/\alpha_i + g_{Fi}$, then $g_{gSi} < 0$. If

$$(23) \qquad g_{Si} = \frac{g_{Mi}}{\alpha_i} + g_{Fi}$$

then $g_{gSi} = 0$. Finally if $g_{Si} < g_{Mi}/\alpha_i + g_{Fi}$, then $g_{gSi} > 0$. Consequently, if greater than (23) g_{Si} is falling; if equal to (23) g_{Si} is stationary; and if less than (23) g_{Si} is rising. Now g_{Si} cannot alternate around (23), for differential equations trace continuous time paths, and as soon as the g_{Si}-path crossed (23) it would have to stay there. Finally g_{Si} cannot converge toward anything else than (23), for if it did, by letting enough time elapse we could make the left-hand side of (22) less than any arbitrarily assignable positive constant, however small, without the same being possible for the right-hand side. A steady-state test, then, has shown that g_{Si} either equals $g_{Mi}/\alpha_i + g_{Fi}$ from the outset or, if it doesn't, will converge toward that value. Insert (23) into (20) and find

$$(24) \qquad g_{Xi} = \frac{g_{Mi}}{\alpha_i} + g_{Fi}$$

Then guess the rest:

$$(25) \qquad g_{Chi} = g_{Xi}$$

$$(26) \qquad g_E = g_{F1} - g_{F2} + g_{w1} - g_{w2}$$

$$(27) \qquad g_{Ii} = g_{Xi}$$

$$(28) \qquad g_{Li} = g_{Fi}$$

$$(29) \qquad g_{Pi} = g_{wi} - \frac{g_{Mi}}{\alpha_i}$$

$$(30) \qquad g_{Yi} = g_{Fi} + g_{wi}$$

To convince himself that those are indeed solutions, the reader should take derivatives with respect to time of (9) through (19). He should then use the definitions (1) through (8), insert the solutions (23) through (30), and convince himself that each equation is satisfied.

4. Unbalanced Growth

By balanced growth we meant identical proportionate rates of growth of physical output for all goods. In (24) neither the rate of technological progress g_{Mi}, nor the labor elasticity of output α_i, nor the rate of growth of labor force g_{Fi} need be equal in the two countries. Consequently we expect no growth balance.

It does however follow from (24), (26), and (29) that when measured in Country 1's monetary unit, the money value of output $P_1 X_1$ and $EP_2 X_2$ of the two countries will indeed be growing at the common rate $g_{F1} + g_{w1}$. What makes this possible is the flexible exchange rate E. According to (26) the rate of growth of the exchange rate equals the difference between the rates of growth of the labor forces *plus* the difference between the rates of growth of the money wage rates. If the former difference were ignored and the latter difference taken to represent the difference between the rates of growth of prices, the purchasing-power-parity theory of the exchange rate would emerge. In our model both steps are inadmissible, but under very brisk inflation both might be justified as crude approximations. Yeager [11] successfully applied the purchasing-power-parity theory to the unruly period 1937–1957.

Notes

[1] Ball, R. J., and K. Mavwah, "The U.S. Demand for Imports, 1948–1958," *Rev. Econ. Stat.*, Nov. 1962, **44,** 395–401.

[2] Bardhan, P. K., "Equilibrium Growth in the International Economy," *Quart. Jour. Econ.*, Aug. 1965, **79,** 455–464.

[3] Brems, H., *Quantitative Economic Theory*, New York, 1968.

[4] Graham, F. D., "The Theory of International Values Re-Examined," *Quart. Jour. Econ.*, Nov. 1923, **38,** 54–86.

[5] Harberger, A. C., "Some Evidence on the International Price Mechanism," *Jour. Pol. Econ.*, Dec. 1957, **65,** 506–522.

[6] Hahn, F. H., and R. C. O. Matthews, "The Theory of Economic Growth: A Survey," *Econ. Jour.*, Dec. 1964, **74,** 779–902.

[7] Houthakker, H. S., and S. P. Magee, "Income and Price Elasticities in World Trade," *Rev. Econ. Stat.*, May 1969, **51,** 111–125.

[8] Kreinin, M., "Price Elasticities in International Trade," *Rev. Econ. Stat.*, Nov. 1967, **49,** 510–516.

[9] Samuelson, P. A., "Using Full Duality to Show that Simultaneously Additive Direct and Indirect Utilities Implies Unitary Price Elasticity of Demand," *Econometrica*, Oct. 1965, **33,** 781–796.

[10] Solow, R. M., and P. A. Samuelson, "Balanced Growth under Constant Returns to Scale," *Econometrica*, July 1953, **21,** 412–424.

[11] Yeager, L. B., "A Rehabilitation of Purchasing-Power Parity," *Jour. Pol. Econ.*, Dec. 1958, **66,** 516–530.

7

Steady-State
Unbalanced
International Growth:
Investment

The second step towards the full-fledged allocation model of Chapter 8 is to let capital move internationally in the form of international direct investment. Define such investment as the movement of a bundle of money capital *plus* technological and managerial knowledge from a domestic parent firm to its foreign subsidiary.[a] In this form money capital is known[b] to flow more easily and in larger volume than in the form of portfolio investment. An additional allocation problem now arises: How do a country's entrepreneurs allocate their investment between domestic parent firm and foreign subsidiary?

An international model must have at least two countries in it. Since international direct investment generates a foreign-owned sector in the host country, each country may have two sectors in it, a domestically-owned and a foreign-owned one. We build our four-sector model as follows. In the ith country let the jth country's entrepreneurs produce a unique good whose output is X_{ij}. In neoclassical tradition [8] this good is produced from, first, the ith country's labor employed by the jth country's entrepreneurs L_{ij}, second, an immortal capital stock S_{ij} of that good. An act of investment I_{ij} by the jth country's entrepreneurs in the ith country is an act of setting aside part of their output there[c] for installation there. If the ith and the jth country are not the same country, that act is an act of international direct investment. The jth country's entrepreneurs allocate their investment between parent firm and foreign subsidiary such as to maximize the present worth of all their future profits. Let the four goods be good, but not perfect, substitutes in

---

[a] Few growth models incorporate international trade, fewer still international investment, and none international direct investment: Borts [1] and Borts and Stein [2] considered a one-country (one-region) open economy in which capital movements are induced by an external disturbance of its equilibrium growth path, hence are no part of growth equilibrium. Hamada [4] considered capital movements part of a growth equilibrium in a two-country model having only one good and one production function in it. These assumptions kill everything distinguishing direct from portfolio investment.

[b] At the end of 1967 the accumulated United States private direct investment abroad was 2.7 times larger than accumulated private long-term portfolio investment [6].

[c] Our assumption that investment is always investment in locally produced goods is realistic: In 1964 the export of capital equipment from the United States to foreign affiliates for use in their own investment programs was merely one-twentieth of the plant and equipment expenditure of those foreign affiliates [7], 13.

consumption, and let each country's consumers have a taste for all four of them. Let C_{hij} be the eight consumptions in the hth country of goods produced in the ith country by the jth country's entrepreneurs.

The money wage rate w_i specified for the ith country is the same in the domestically-owned and the foreign-owned sector of that country. The two national money wage rates are parameters. But the four goods prices P_{ij} are variables, consequently the real wage rate in terms of any of the four goods is also a variable. Furthermore, the exchange rate is a variable. Such reliance

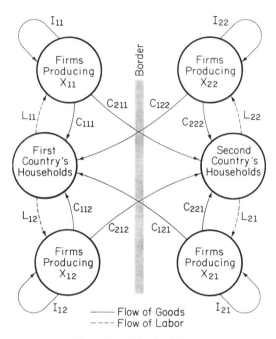

Figure 7-1. Physical flows.

on the price mechanism enables us to specify equilibrium conditions for each national labor market, each of the four goods markets, and the balance of payments. The latter includes international trade, international investment, and repatriation of profits. Figure 7-1 shows all physical flows and Figure 7-2 all money flows in our model.

Section I defines variables and parameters. Section II specifies the model mathematically. Section III finds equilibrium solutions for growth rates, and

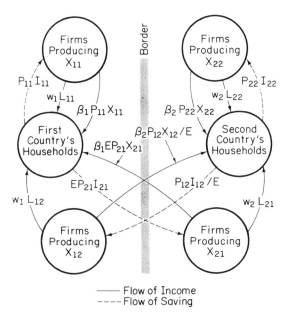

Figure 7-2. Money flows.

Section IV finds equilibrium solutions for levels of important variables. Section V offers four numerical examples of our equilibrium solution illustrating United States direct investment abroad. Conclusions are drawn in Section VI.

I. Notation

Variables

C_{hij} ≡ consumption in hth country of goods produced in ith country by jth country's entrepreneurs

E ≡ exchange rate in number of monetary units of Country 1 exchanged for one monetary unit of Country 2

ϕ ≡ function to be maximized by the Lagrange-multiplier method

g_v ≡ proportionate rate of growth of variable v where $v ≡ C, E, I, L, P, S, X,$ and Y

I_{ij} ≡ investment by jth country's entrepreneurs in ith country

$\kappa_{ij} \equiv$ physical marginal productivity of capital stock in ith country owned by jth country's entrepreneurs

$L_{ij} \equiv i$th country's labor employed by jth country's entrepreneurs

$P_{ij} \equiv$ price of good produced in ith country by jth country's entrepreneurs, expressed in ith country's monetary unit

$R_j \equiv$ sum of sector revenues of jth country's entrepreneurs

$S_{ij} \equiv$ capital stock of goods produced in ith country by jth country's entrepreneurs

$U_{ik} \equiv$ utility to kth person in ith country

$W_i \equiv i$th country's wage bill

$X_{ij} \equiv$ output of good produced in ith country by jth country's entrepreneurs

$Y_i \equiv i$th country's national money income

$Z_j \equiv$ current profits of jth country's entrepreneurs

$\zeta_j \equiv$ present worth of all future profits of jth country's entrepreneurs

Parameters

$A_{hij} \equiv$ parameters of individual utility function in hth country

$\alpha_j, \beta_j \equiv$ parameters of production function of jth country's entrepreneurs

$c_i \equiv i$th country's propensity to consume its national money income

$F_i \equiv i$th country's available labor force

$g_p \equiv$ proportionate rate of growth of parameter p where $p \equiv F, M,$ and w

$\lambda \equiv$ Lagrange multiplier

$M_j \equiv$ multiplicative factor in production function of jth country's entrepreneurs

$N_i \equiv$ multiplicative factor in utility function in ith country

$r_j \equiv$ discount rate applied by jth country's entrepreneurs

$w_i \equiv i$th country's money wage rate

Subscripts $i = 1, 2$ and $j = 1, 2$ refer to country number.

All flow variables refer to the instantaneous rate of that variable measured on a per annum basis. The parameters listed are stationary except F, M, and w, whose proportionate rates of growth are stationary. Symbols t and τ are time coordinates. The symbol e is Euler's number, the base of natural logarithms. Symbols D, h, m, q, and π stand for agglomerations of variables and parameters and will be defined as we go along.

II. The Equations of the Model

In Section I, 31 variable growth rates are listed, i.e., eight growth rates of C_{hij}; one growth rate of E; four growth rates of each of I_{ij}, L_{ij}, P_{ij}, S_{ij}, and X_{ij}; and two growth rates of Y_i. To all apply the definition

(1) through (31)
$$g_v \equiv \frac{dv}{dt} \frac{1}{v}$$

Define investment as the derivative of capital stock with respect to time:

(32) through (35)
$$I_{ij} \equiv \frac{dS_{ij}}{dt}$$

When producing in the ith country, let the jth country's entrepreneurs apply the Cobb-Douglas production function

(36) through (39)
$$X_{ij} = M_j L_{ij}{}^{\alpha_j} S_{ij}{}^{\beta_j}$$

where $0 < \alpha_j < 1$, $0 < \beta_j < 1$, $\alpha_j + \beta_j = 1$, and $M_j > 0$. While the jth country's entrepreneurs do not produce the same good at home and abroad, their α_j, β_j, and M_j are the same: If disposed at home toward highly automated methods, they will be so disposed in their foreign subsidiaries as well. Technological progress made at home will be applied in the foreign subsidiaries as well.

In any sector let profit maximization under pure competition equalize real wage rate and physical marginal productivity of labor:

(40) through (43)
$$\frac{w_i}{P_{ij}} = \frac{\partial X_{ij}}{\partial L_{ij}} = \alpha_j \frac{X_{ij}}{L_{ij}}$$

Define the physical marginal productivity of capital as

(44) through (47)
$$\kappa_{ij} \equiv \frac{\partial X_{ij}}{\partial S_{ij}} = \beta_j \frac{X_{ij}}{S_{ij}}$$

Define the revenue of the jth country's entrepreneurs as

(48)
$$R_1 \equiv P_{11}X_{11} + EP_{21}X_{21}$$

(49)
$$R_2 \equiv \frac{P_{12}X_{12}}{E} + P_{22}X_{22}$$

It follows from (44) through (47) applied to (48) and (49) that at time t the jth country's entrepreneurs will be earning the profits

(50), (51)
$$Z_j(t) = \beta_j R_j(t)$$

As seen from time τ these profits are

$$Z_j(t, \tau) \equiv Z_j(t)e^{-r_j(t-\tau)}$$

where r_j is the discount rate applied by the jth country's entrepreneurs. The present worth of all future profits as seen from time τ is

(52), (53)
$$\zeta_j(\tau) \equiv \int_\tau^\infty Z_j(t)e^{-r_j(t-\tau)}\, dt$$

Let the jth country's entrepreneurs allocate their investment between parent firm and foreign subsidiary such that

(54), (55)
$$\zeta_j(\tau) = \text{maximum}$$

Under full employment the ith country's available labor force must equal the sum of labor employed by the jth country's entrepreneurs operating in the ith country:

(56), (57)
$$F_i = \sum_{j=1}^{2} L_{ij}$$

Define the ith country's wage bill as its money wage rate *times* its combined employment:

(58),(59)
$$W_i \equiv w_i \sum_{j=1}^{2} L_{ij}$$

Define the jth country's national money income as the sum of its wage bill and the profits bill earned by its entrepreneurs:

(60), (61)
$$Y_j \equiv W_j + Z_j$$

Within each country let all persons have the same utility function, but let the latter differ between countries. Let the utility function of the kth person in the hth country be

$$U_{1k} = N_1 C_{111k}^{A_{111}} C_{112k}^{A_{112}} C_{121k}^{A_{121}} C_{122k}^{A_{122}}$$

$$U_{2k} = N_2 C_{211k}^{A_{211}} C_{212k}^{A_{212}} C_{221k}^{A_{221}} C_{222k}^{A_{222}}$$

where $0 < A_{hij} < 1$ and $N_h > 0$. In the hth country let there be s_h persons, and let the kth person's money income be Y_{hk} where

$$\sum_{k=1}^{s_h} Y_{hk} = Y_h$$

Let all persons in the hth country spend the fraction c_h, where $0 < c_h < 1$, of their money income on consumption. Then the budget constraint of the kth person in the hth country is

$$c_i Y_{1k} = P_{11}C_{111k} + P_{12}C_{112k} + E(P_{21}C_{121k} + P_{22}C_{122k})$$

$$c_2 Y_{2k} = \frac{P_{11}C_{211k} + P_{12}C_{212k}}{E} + P_{21}C_{221k} + P_{22}C_{222k}$$

Maximize the kth person's utility subject to his budget constraint and find his four demand functions. For each country add the s_h individual demand functions for each good and find the four Graham-type[d] [3] demand functions

$$(62) \qquad C_{111} = \frac{\pi_{111}Y_1}{P_{11}}$$

$$(63) \qquad C_{112} = \frac{\pi_{112}Y_1}{P_{12}}$$

$$(64) \qquad C_{121} = \frac{\pi_{121}Y_1}{EP_{21}}$$

$$(65) \qquad C_{122} = \frac{\pi_{122}Y_1}{EP_{22}}$$

$$(66) \qquad C_{211} = \frac{\pi_{211}EY_2}{P_{11}}$$

$$(67) \qquad C_{212} = \frac{\pi_{212}EY_2}{P_{12}}$$

$$(68) \qquad C_{221} = \frac{\pi_{221}Y_2}{P_{21}}$$

$$(69) \qquad C_{222} = \frac{\pi_{222}Y_2}{P_{22}}$$

where

$$\pi_{hij} \equiv \frac{c_h A_{hij}}{A_{h11} + A_{h12} + A_{h21} + A_{h22}}$$

---

[d] For empirical income and price elasticities of import demand, see Footnote c of Chapter 6.

Sector output equilibrium requires the output in the ith country produced by the jth country's entrepreneurs to equal the sum of consumption, export, and investment demand for it, or inventory would either accumulate or be depleted. Thus

$$(70) \text{ through } (73) \qquad X_{ij} = \sum_{h=1}^{2} C_{hij} + I_{ij}$$

Balance-of-payments equilibrium requires Country 1's consumption of and investment in Country 2's goods *minus* Country 1's profits earned in Country 2, to equal Country 2's consumption of and investment in Country 1's goods *minus* Country 2's profits earned in Country 1, all being measured in the same monetary unit. If this equality were not satisfied, exchange reserves of the ith country would either accumulate or be depleted. Thus

$$(74) \qquad E(P_{21}C_{121} + P_{22}C_{122} + P_{21}I_{21} - \beta_1 P_{21}X_{21})$$
$$= P_{11}C_{211} + P_{12}C_{212} + P_{12}I_{12} - \beta_2 P_{12}X_{12}$$

III. Solutions for Proportionate Rates of Growth

Our system (1) through (74) possesses the following set of steady-state solutions for its 31 equilibrium rates of growth:

(75) through (82) $\quad g_{Chij} = g_{Xij}$

(83) $\qquad g_E = g_{F1} - g_{F2} + g_{w1} - g_{w2}$

(84) through (87) $\quad g_{Iij} = g_{Xij}$

(88) through (91) $\quad g_{Lij} = g_{Fi}$

(92) through (95) $\quad g_{Pij} = g_{wi} - \dfrac{g_{Mj}}{\alpha_j}$

(96) through (99) $\quad g_{Sij} = g_{Xij}$

(100) through (103) $\quad g_{Xij} = \dfrac{g_{Mj}}{\alpha_j} + g_{Fi}$

(104), (105) $\qquad g_{Yi} = g_{Fi} + g_{wi}$

To convince himself that those are indeed solutions, the reader should take derivatives with respect to time of all equations (32) through (43), (48) and (49), and (56) through (74), then use definitions (1) through (31), insert solutions (75) through (105), and convince himself that each equation is satisfied.

We defined balanced growth as identical proportionate rates of growth of physical output for all goods. According to our solutions (75) through (105), is our steady-state growth balanced or unbalanced? In (100) through (103) neither g_{Mj}/α_j nor g_{Fi} can be expected to be identical in all four sectors. For example, if, other things being equal, the entrepreneurs of one country had a higher g_{Mj} than those of the other country, the physical outputs offered by the technological leaders would be growing more rapidly than those offered by the laggards, and growth would be unbalanced—as it is in the real world.

It does, however, follow from (83), (92) through (95), and (100) through (103) that when measured in Country 1's monetary unit, all four revenues $P_{ij}X_{ij}$ will be growing at the same proportionate rate $g_{F1} + g_{w1}$.

IV. Solutions for Levels

Second, we solve for the equilibrium levels at a particular time of the exchange rate, revenues, national incomes, marginal productivities of capital, foreign direct investments, and net national capital export. To do so we need a *numéraire* for each country. According to (56) through (59) the ith country's wage bill in terms of parameters is $W_i = F_i w_i$. Let us use the wage bills W_i for our *numéraires*.

1. A Country's Saving Equals Direct Investment by its Entrepreneurs

Multiply each of the sector-output equilibrium conditions (70) through (73) by its price P_{ij} expressed in the same country's monetary unit for all four of them. Add the conditions for $ij = 11$, 12 and subtract (74) from their sum. Add the conditions for $ij = 21$, 22 and add (74) to their sum. Use (40) through (43), (48), (49), and (56) through (69) and find:

$$(106) \qquad (1 - c_1)Y_1 = P_{11}I_{11} + EP_{21}I_{21}$$

$$(107) \qquad (1 - c_2)EY_2 = P_{12}I_{12} + EP_{22}I_{22}$$

Are (106) and (107) trivial? Clearly not, for in general an open economy's saving equals the sum of the direct investment by its entrepreneurs in parent firm and foreign subsidiary *plus* the net change in the country's exchange reserves. But thanks to our equilibrium condition (74) that net change is zero.

2. *Present-Worth Maximization*

Subject to the constraints (106) and (107), let the jth country's entrepreneurs use their control variable I_{ij} to optimize the allocation of their capital stock S_{ij} between parent firm and foreign subsidiary. "Optimize" in what sense? In the sense of maximizing the present worth $\zeta_j(\tau)$ of all future profits bills in accordance with (54) and (55). Using (48) through (53) we write present worth for the first country's entrepreneurs as

$$(108) \quad \zeta_1(\tau) = \int_\tau^\infty \beta_1[P_{11}(t)X_{11}(t) + E(t)P_{21}(t)X_{21}(t)]e^{-r_j(t-\tau)}\, dt$$

Let it be foreseen by the entrepreneurs that prices are growing in accordance with our steady-state solutions (92) through (95), hence

$$(109),\ (110) \qquad\qquad P_{ij}(t) = e^{g_{Pij}(t-\tau)}P_{ij}(\tau)$$

that outputs are growing in accordance with our steady-state solutions (100) through (103), hence

$$(111),\ (112) \qquad\qquad X_{ij}(t) = e^{g_{Xij}(t-\tau)}X_{ij}(\tau)$$

and that the exchange rate is growing in accordance with our steady-state solution (83), hence

$$(113) \qquad\qquad E(t) = e^{g_E(t-\tau)}E(\tau)$$

Consequently we may take prices, outputs, and the exchange rate outside the integral sign and write present worth as

$$(114) \quad \zeta_1(\tau) = \beta_1 P_{11}(\tau)X_{11}(\tau)\int_\tau^\infty e^{(g_{P11}+g_{X11}-r_1)(t-\tau)}\, dt$$

$$+\ \beta_1 E(\tau)P_{21}(\tau)X_{21}(\tau)\int_\tau^\infty e^{(g_E+g_{P21}+g_{X21}-r_1)(t-\tau)}\, dt$$

Since in this expression all variables refer to the same time τ, we may purge it of τ. Use (83), (92) through (95), and (100) through (103) to see that

$$(115) \qquad g_{P11} + g_{X11} = g_E + g_{P21} + g_{X21} = g_{F1} + g_{w1}$$

Assume that $g_{F1} + g_{w1} < r_1$, then integrate:

$$(116) \qquad\qquad \zeta_1 = \frac{\beta_1(P_{11}X_{11} + EP_{21}X_{21})}{r_1 - (g_{F1} + g_{w1})}$$

Inserting (48) through (51) into (116) we find the simple relationship between profits and present worth under steady-state growth:

(117) $$Z_1 = [r_1 - (g_{F1} + g_{w1})]\zeta_1$$

Maximizing present worth ζ_1 subject to the constraint (106) is most easily done by using a Lagrange multiplier: Define a new function to be maximized

(118) $$\phi_1 = \zeta_1 + \lambda[(1 - c_1)Y_1 - (P_{11}I_{11} + EP_{21}I_{21})]$$

What to do with Y? Insert (117) into (60), insert the outcome into ϕ_1 and write the latter

(119) $$\phi_1 = \{1 + \lambda(1 - c_1)[r_1 - (g_{F1} + g_{w1})]\}\zeta_1$$
$$+ \lambda(1 - c_1)W_1 - \lambda(P_{11}I_{11} + EP_{21}I_{21})$$

The first two first-order conditions for a maximum ϕ_1 are

(120) $$\frac{\partial\phi_1}{\partial I_{11}} = h_{11}\frac{\partial X_{11}}{\partial I_{11}} - \lambda P_{11} = 0$$

(121) $$\frac{\partial\phi_1}{\partial I_{21}} = h_{21}\frac{\partial X_{21}}{\partial I_{21}} - \lambda EP_{21} = 0$$

where

$$h_{11} \equiv \frac{\{1 + \lambda(1 - c_1)[r_1 - (g_{F1} + g_{w1})]\}\beta_1 P_{11}}{r_1 - (g_{F1} + g_{w1})}$$

$$h_{21} \equiv \frac{\{1 + \lambda(1 - c_1)[r_1 - (g_{F1} + g_{w1})]\}\beta_1 EP_{21}}{r_1 - (g_{F1} + g_{w1})}$$

Now according to the production functions (36) through (39), output X_{ij} is a function of capital stock S_{ij} rather than of investment I_{ij}. But according to (1) through (35):

(122), (123) $$S_{ij} \equiv \frac{I_{ij}}{g_{Sij}}$$

where our steady-state growth, as specified by (96) through (103), permits us to express g_{Sij} solely in terms of parameters. Inserting (122) and (123) into the production functions (36) through (39) we find

(124), (125) $$\frac{\partial X_{ij}}{\partial I_{ij}} = \beta_j \frac{X_{ij}}{I_{ij}}$$

and write the first-order conditions for both countries' entrepreneurs as

$$
(126) \qquad \frac{X_{11}}{I_{11}} = \frac{X_{21}}{I_{21}} = \frac{\lambda[r_1 - (g_{F1} + g_{w1})]}{\{1 + \lambda(1 - c_1)[r_1 - (g_{F1} + g_{w1})]\}\beta_1{}^2}
$$

$$
(127) \qquad \frac{X_{12}}{I_{12}} = \frac{X_{22}}{I_{22}} = \frac{\lambda[r_2 - (g_{F2} + g_{w2})]}{\{1 + \lambda(1 - c_2)[r_2 - (g_{F2} + g_{w2})]\}\beta_2{}^2}
$$

That the second-order conditions are satisfied is demonstrated in the Appendix.

3. *Sector Revenues*

Divide each of the sector-output equilibrium conditions (70) through (73) by output X_{ij}. Express the difference between the conditions for $ij = 11, 21$, use (126) and find that

$$
\frac{C_{111} + C_{211}}{X_{11}} = \frac{C_{121} + C_{221}}{X_{21}}
$$

Next express the difference between the conditions for $ij = 12, 22$, use (127) and find that

$$
\frac{C_{112} + C_{212}}{X_{12}} = \frac{C_{122} + C_{222}}{X_{22}}
$$

Multiply each of the sector-output equilibrium conditions (70) through (73) by its price P_{ij} expressed in the same country's monetary unit for all four of them. Add the conditions for $ij = 11, 21$, using (48) and (106). Next add the conditions for $ij = 12, 22$, using (49) and (107). Use results above, insert (62) through (69), and find

$$
(128) \qquad P_{11}X_{11} = \frac{(\pi_{111}Y_1 + \pi_{211}EY_2)R_1}{(\pi_{111} + \pi_{121})Y_1 + (\pi_{211} + \pi_{221})EY_2}
$$

$$
(129) \qquad P_{12}X_{12} = \frac{(\pi_{112}Y_1 + \pi_{212}EY_2)ER_2}{(\pi_{112} + \pi_{122})Y_1 + (\pi_{212} + \pi_{222})EY_2}
$$

$$
(130) \qquad EP_{21}X_{21} = \frac{(\pi_{121}Y_1 + \pi_{221}EY_2)R_1}{(\pi_{111} + \pi_{121})Y_1 + (\pi_{211} + \pi_{221})EY_2}
$$

$$
(131) \qquad EP_{22}X_{22} = \frac{(\pi_{122}Y_1 + \pi_{222}EY_2)ER_2}{(\pi_{112} + \pi_{122})Y_1 + (\pi_{212} + \pi_{222})EY_2}
$$

Once again use (70) through (73), (48) and (49), (106) and (107), and (62) through (69), but this time insert (50), (51), (60), and (61) and find

$$(132) \qquad R_1 = q_1 W_1 + q_2 EW_2$$

$$(133) \qquad ER_2 = q_3 W_1 + q_4 EW_2$$

where

$$q_1 \equiv \frac{\alpha_2[1 - (\pi_{112} + \pi_{122})] + \beta_2(\pi_{211} + \pi_{221})}{D}$$

$$q_2 \equiv \frac{\pi_{211} + \pi_{221}}{D}$$

$$q_3 \equiv \frac{\pi_{112} + \pi_{122}}{D}$$

$$q_4 \equiv \frac{\alpha_1[1 - (\pi_{211} + \pi_{221})] + \beta_1(\pi_{112} + \pi_{122})}{D}$$

$$D \equiv \alpha_1\alpha_2 + \alpha_2\beta_1(\pi_{112} + \pi_{122}) + \alpha_1\beta_2(\pi_{211} + \pi_{221})$$

Use (40) through (43) together with (56) through (59) to express the national wage bills as

$$(134) \qquad W_1 = \alpha_1 P_{11} X_{11} + \alpha_2 P_{12} X_{12}$$

$$(135) \qquad W_2 = \alpha_1 P_{21} X_{21} + \alpha_2 P_{22} X_{22}$$

4. Solving for the Exchange Rate

At long last we are now able to reduce our nonlinear system (1) through (74) to one cubic equation in one variable. To simplify that equation define an auxiliary variable

$$(136) \qquad x \equiv \frac{EW_2}{W_1}$$

We may now insert (50), (51), (60), (61), (132), and (133) into (128) and (129), insert the results into (134), use (136), and get the cubic equation in our new unknown x:

$$
\begin{aligned}
(137) \quad & [m_1 + m_5 + (m_2 + m_6)x][m_3 + m_7 + (m_4 + m_8)x] \\
& = \alpha_1(q_1 + q_2 x)(m_1 + m_2 x)[m_3 + m_7 + (m_4 + m_8)x] \\
& \quad + \alpha_2(q_3 + q_4 x)(m_3 + m_4 x)[m_1 + m_5 + (m_2 + m_6)x]
\end{aligned}
$$

If instead we had inserted (50), (51), (60), (61), (132) and (133) into (130) and (131), had inserted the results into (135) and used (136), we would have arrived at another cubic equation in our new unknown x:

$$
\begin{aligned}
(138) \quad & x[m_1 + m_5 + (m_2 + m_6)x][m_3 + m_7 + (m_4 + m_8)x] \\
& = \alpha_1(q_1 + q_2x)(m_5 + m_6x)[m_3 + m_7 + (m_4 + m_8)x] \\
& \quad + \alpha_2(q_3 + q_4x)(m_7 + m_8x)[m_1 + m_5 + (m_2 + m_6)x]
\end{aligned}
$$

where

$$
\begin{aligned}
m_1 &\equiv \pi_{111}(1 + \beta_1 q_1) + \pi_{211}\beta_2 q_3 \\
m_2 &\equiv \pi_{211}(1 + \beta_2 q_4) + \pi_{111}\beta_1 q_2 \\
m_3 &\equiv \pi_{112}(1 + \beta_1 q_1) + \pi_{212}\beta_2 q_3 \\
m_4 &\equiv \pi_{212}(1 + \beta_2 q_4) + \pi_{112}\beta_1 q_2 \\
m_5 &\equiv \pi_{121}(1 + \beta_1 q_1) + \pi_{221}\beta_2 q_3 \\
m_6 &\equiv \pi_{221}(1 + \beta_2 q_4) + \pi_{121}\beta_1 q_2 \\
m_7 &\equiv \pi_{122}(1 + \beta_1 q_1) + \pi_{222}\beta_2 q_3 \\
m_8 &\equiv \pi_{222}(1 + \beta_2 q_4) + \pi_{122}\beta_1 q_2
\end{aligned}
$$

5. Solving for the Marginal Productivities of Capital

Use the definitions (44) through (47) and (1) through (35) to express the marginal productivities of capital in terms of the ratio X_{ij}/I_{ij}. Then use (50), (51), (60) through (73) and (128) through (133) to express that ratio and find

$$
(139) \quad \kappa_{11} = \frac{\beta_1 g_{S11}}{1 - [(m_1 + m_5)W_1 + (m_2 + m_6)EW_2]/(q_1 W_1 + q_2 EW_2)}
$$

$$
(140) \quad \kappa_{12} = \frac{\beta_2 g_{S12}}{1 - [(m_3 + m_7)W_1 + (m_4 + m_8)EW_2]/(q_3 W_1 + q_4 EW_2)}
$$

$$
(141) \quad \kappa_{21} = \frac{\beta_1 g_{S21}}{1 - [(m_1 + m_5)W_1 + (m_2 + m_6)EW_2]/(q_1 W_1 + q_2 EW_2)}
$$

$$
(142) \quad \kappa_{22} = \frac{\beta_2 g_{S22}}{1 - [(m_3 + m_7)W_1 + (m_4 + m_8)EW_2]/(q_3 W_1 + q_4 EW_2)}
$$

6. *Solving for Net National Capital Export*

First use the definitions (44) through (47) and (1) through (35) to express investment in terms of output and (139) through (142):

$$(143) \qquad P_{12}I_{12} = \frac{P_{12}X_{12}\beta_2 g_{S12}}{\kappa_{12}}$$

$$(144) \qquad EP_{21}I_{21} = \frac{EP_{21}X_{21}\beta_1 g_{S21}}{\kappa_{21}}$$

Second, recall that Eqs. (106) and (107) defined the savings of Country 1 and Country 2, respectively. The combined investments undertaken within those countries are, respectively

$$(145) \qquad P_{11}I_{11} + P_{12}I_{12}$$

$$(146) \qquad EP_{21}I_{21} + EP_{22}I_{22}$$

Now deduct (145) from (106) and find Country 1's excess of saving over investment within it or, which is the same thing, Country 1's net national capital export

$$(147) \qquad EP_{21}I_{21} - P_{12}I_{12}$$

Had we deducted (146) from (107) we would have found Country 2's net national capital export equalling, of course, (147) with opposite sign.

7. *Collapsing our System*

We have succeeded in reducing our nonlinear system (1) through (74) to one cubic equation in one variable—of the form (137) or (138). But the cubic equation is a formidable one, and relief would be welcome. Relief can be had by assuming that in the consumer's utility function the exponents A_{hij} of the consumptions C_{hij} of the two goods produced by the jth country's entrepreneurs are the same. If so, then in the demand equations (62) through (69) we have

$$(148) \qquad \pi_{111} = \pi_{121}$$

$$(149) \qquad \pi_{112} = \pi_{122}$$

$$(150) \qquad \pi_{211} = \pi_{221}$$

$$(151) \qquad \pi_{212} = \pi_{222}$$

What is the economic implication of such strong assumptions—made uncomfortably? The two goods produced by the jth country's entrepreneurs are not only produced under production functions having the same parameters α_j, β_j, and M_j, they are now also assumed to be raised to the same power A_{hij} in the utility function in the hth country. Are they, then, identical goods? Is our four-good model now collapsing into a two-good model? The answer is no, for the two goods are still not perfect substitutes, hence may sell side by side at different prices.

We could live with our four new assumptions (148) through (151) if our main interest were the relative success of one country's entrepreneurs vis-à-vis those of the other—the American Challenge. But why *should* we live with them? What is the use of such strong assumptions? Their effect is to make $m_1 = m_5$, $m_2 = m_6$, $m_3 = m_7$, and $m_4 = m_8$. One might then divide (138) by (137) and get the linear equation $x = 1$. Such linearity would enable us to find the following drastically simplified solutions for the levels of the exchange rate, revenues, national incomes, marginal productivities of capital, foreign direct investments, and net national capital export. Use (136) to find the exchange rate

$$(152) \qquad E = \frac{W_1}{W_2}$$

Insert (152) into (132) and (133) and find the combined sector revenues

$$(153) \qquad R_1 = (q_1 + q_2)W_1$$

$$(154) \qquad ER_2 = (q_3 + q_4)W_1$$

Insert (148) through (151), (153), and (154) into (128) through (131) and find the four sector revenues collapsing into

$$(155) \qquad P_{11}X_{11} = \frac{(q_1 + q_2)W_1}{2}$$

$$(156) \qquad P_{12}X_{12} = \frac{(q_3 + q_4)W_1}{2}$$

$$(157) \qquad EP_{21}X_{21} = \frac{(q_1 + q_2)W_1}{2}$$

$$(158) \qquad EP_{22}X_{22} = \frac{(q_3 + q_4)W_1}{2}$$

Insert (50) and (51), (153) and (154) into (60) and (61) and find national money incomes

$$(159) \qquad Y_1 = [1 + \beta_1(q_1 + q_2)]W_1$$

$$(160) \qquad EY_2 = [1 + \beta_2(q_3 + q_4)]W_1$$

Insert (148) through (152) into (139) through (142) and find the four marginal productivities of capital

$$(161) \qquad \kappa_{11} = \frac{\beta_1 g_{s11}}{1 - 2(m_1 + m_2)/(q_1 + q_2)}$$

$$(162) \qquad \kappa_{12} = \frac{\beta_2 g_{s12}}{1 - 2(m_3 + m_4)/(q_3 + q_4)}$$

$$(163) \qquad \kappa_{21} = \frac{\beta_1 g_{s21}}{1 - 2(m_1 + m_2)/(q_1 + q_2)}$$

$$(164) \qquad \kappa_{22} = \frac{\beta_2 g_{s22}}{1 - 2(m_3 + m_4)/(q_3 + q_4)}$$

Finally insert (156), (157), (162), (163) into (143), (144), and (147) and find Country 1's net national capital export to be the difference between the two foreign investments $EP_{21}I_{21} - P_{12}I_{12}$ where

$$P_{12}I_{12} = \frac{[q_3 + q_4 - 2(m_3 + m_4)]W_1}{2}$$

$$EP_{21}I_{21} = \frac{[q_1 + q_2 - 2(m_1 + m_2)]W_1}{2}$$

V. Numerical Examples

1. *Master Case*

To illustrate United States direct investment abroad, Table 7-1 shows four numerical examples of our drastically simplified solutions. The first example is a master case of complete symmetry—hence zero net national capital export—between the two countries, using realistic values of the technology parameters and the propensity to consume, i.e., $\alpha_j = 3/4$, $\beta_j = 1/4$, $c_i = 8/9$, and $\pi_{hij} = 2/9$. Let us now modify our master case.

Table 7-1. Revenues, National Incomes, Marginal Productivities of Capital, Foreign Direct Investments, and Net National Capital Export

Variable		Master Case	Changed Thriftiness Case	Changed Technology Case	Changed Preference Case
Revenues	R_1	$1.33W_1$	$1.39W_1$	$1.42W_1$	$1.94W_1$
	ER_2	$1.33W_1$	$1.27W_1$	$1.41W_1$	$0.72W_1$
National Incomes	Y_1	$1.33W_1$	$1.35W_1$	$1.47W_1$	$1.49W_1$
	EY_2	$1.33W_1$	$1.32W_1$	$1.35W_1$	$1.18W_1$
Marginal Productivities	κ_{i1}	$2.25g_{si1}$	$1.29g_{si1}$	$2.89g_{si1}$	$2.94g_{si1}$
	κ_{i2}	$2.25g_{si2}$	$2.17g_{si2}$	$2.34g_{si2}$	$1.38g_{si2}$
Foreign Direct Investments	$EP_{21}I_{21}$	$0.074W_1$	$0.135W_1$	$0.082W_1$	$0.083W_1$
	$P_{12}I_{12}$	$0.074W_1$	$0.073W_1$	$0.075W_1$	$0.065W_1$
Net National Capital Export		0	$0.062W_1$	$0.007W_1$	$0.017W_1$

2. Changed-Thriftiness Case

United States superiority is sometimes sought in capital abundance. So without changing our master-case technology and preferences let us reduce the propensity to consume of Country 1. For example, assume $\alpha_j = 3/4$, $\beta_j = 1/4$, $c_1 = 4/5$, $c_2 = 8/9$, $\pi_{111} = \pi_{112} = \pi_{121} = \pi_{122} = 1/5$, and $\pi_{211} = \pi_{212} = \pi_{221} = \pi_{222} = 2/9$. Table 7-1 shows that this will reduce the marginal productivities of capital earned by the entrepreneurs of both countries—although in our model the saving of a United States saver never gets inside a European-owned firm. It does, however, get inside United States-owned firms competing with European-owned firms everywhere (the four goods are good, but not perfect, substitutes). Because of its higher thriftiness Country 1 now has a positive net national capital export.

3. Changed-Technology Case

United States superiority is sometimes sought in its knowledge of highly automated production methods. So without changing our master-case preferences and propensity to consume let us make the technology known to the entrepreneurs of Country 1 more automated. For example, assume $\alpha_1 = 2/3$, $\beta_1 = 1/3$, $\alpha_2 = 3/4$, $\beta_2 = 1/4$, $c_i = 8/9$, and $\pi_{hij} = 2/9$. Table 7-1 shows that this will raise all variables of both countries. The marginal productivities of capital earned by the first country's entrepreneurs κ_{i1} are raised for two reasons; first, their coefficient is raised from 2.25 to 2.89, and second, according to (96) through (103) g_{Si1} rises with falling α_1. Because of the superior knowledge of its entrepreneurs Country 1 again has a positive net national capital export.

4. *A Widening Technology Gap*

A technology gap is said to be opening up between the United States and Western Europe, so without changing our master-case exponents α_j and β_j, propensity to consume or preferences, let us asume such a gap to be developing in the form that $g_{M1} > g_{M2}$. Such a gap can affect neither the revenues R_j, the national incomes Y_i, nor the net capital export $EP_{21}I_{21} - P_{12}I_{12}$, for g_{Mj} is absent from the solutions for those variables. But according to (96) through (103) g_{Mj} is indeed present in the solution for g_{Sij} and hence in the solutions (161) through (164) for the marginal productivities of capital κ_{ij}. Consequently the technological leaders will, other things being equal, have higher marginal productivities of capital than the laggards.

5. *Changed-Preference Case*

United States superiority is often sought in management rather than in capital abundance or technology. So at unchanged master-case technology and propensity to consume, let the entrepreneurs of Country 1 have succeeded better than those of Country 2 in conceiving and developing the optimal products. As a result, the preferences for the two goods produced by the entrepreneurs of Country 1 are up, while the preferences for the other two goods are down. For example, assume $\alpha_j = 3/4$, $\beta_j = 1/4$, $c_i = 8/9$, $\pi_{111} = \pi_{121} = \pi_{211} = \pi_{221} = 3/9$, and $\pi_{112} = \pi_{122} = \pi_{212} = \pi_{222} = 1/9$. Table 7-1 shows that this will raise the marginal productivities earned by the first country's entrepreneurs and reduce those earned by the second country's entrepreneurs. Country 1 again has a positive net national capital export.

VI. Conclusions

We have built and solved a four-sector growth model of international direct investment. Define steady-state growth as stationary proportionate rates of growth, and balanced growth as identical proportionate rates of growth of physical sector outputs X_{ij}. Unlike most growth models, our model real-listically generates steady-state but unbalanced growth: The physical outputs of the four sectors may well be growing at four different proportionate rates. If there is an American Challenge in our model, this is it.

Capital movements in the form of two-way international direct investment are a permanent, realistic,[e] and nonparadoxical feature of our full equilibrium. One country's entrepreneurs may simply be superior in computers, those of the other in steel. Once our two-way international direct investment flows are determined, so is their net. The direction of the net depends of course upon the entire structure of the model. To illustrate this, we first offered a numerical example of complete symmetry—and hence zero net national capital export—between the two countries. We then broke the symmetry by assuming Country 1 superior in terms of either thriftiness, technology, or consumer preference for the products offered by its entrepreneurs. In all three cases, its net national capital export changed from zero to positive, and in this sense thriftiness, technology, or management each may contribute to an explanation of United States direct investment abroad.

---

[e] Measured in billions of dollars per annum, the outward and inward flows of direct investment were for the United States during 1967 4.6 and 0.9, respectively [6], 22; for West Germany during 1967 0.25 and 0.70, respectively [9], 64*; and for Sweden on an average 1961-1965 0.068 and 0.056, respectively [5], 135.

Write the bordered Hessian

(165)
$$H \equiv \begin{vmatrix} \dfrac{\partial^2 \phi_1}{\partial I_{11}{}^2} & \dfrac{\partial^2 \phi_1}{\partial I_{11}\partial I_{21}} & -P_{11} \\[3mm] \dfrac{\partial^2 \phi_1}{\partial I_{21}\partial I_{11}} & \dfrac{\partial^2 \phi_1}{\partial I_{21}{}^2} & -EP_{21} \\[3mm] -P_{11} & -EP_{21} & 0 \end{vmatrix}$$

The first derivatives $\partial\phi_1/\partial I_{ij}$ have already been taken and were of the form (120) and (121). It follows from that form that two of the second derivatives contained in our Hessian are zero: After inserting (122) and (123) into our production functions (36) through (39) we realize that X_{11} is not a function of I_{21} and X_{21} not a function of I_{11}, hence

$$\frac{\partial X_{11}}{\partial I_{21}} = \frac{\partial X_{21}}{\partial I_{11}} = \frac{\partial^2 X_{11}}{\partial I_{21}\partial I_{11}} = \frac{\partial^2 X_{21}}{\partial I_{11}\partial I_{21}} = 0$$

But X_{ij} is a function of I_{ij}, hence using (120) through (127) we find

$$\frac{\partial^2 \phi_1}{\partial I_{11}{}^2} = \frac{(\beta_1 - 1)\lambda P_{11}}{I_{11}}$$

$$\frac{\partial^2 \phi_1}{\partial I_{21}{}^2} = \frac{(\beta_1 - 1)\lambda EP_{21}}{I_{21}}$$

Consequently our Hessian (165) is

$$H = \begin{vmatrix} \dfrac{(\beta_1 - 1)\lambda P_{11}}{I_{11}} & 0 & -P_{11} \\[3mm] 0 & \dfrac{(\beta_1 - 1)\lambda EP_{21}}{I_{21}} & -EP_{21} \\[3mm] -P_{11} & -EP_{21} & 0 \end{vmatrix}$$

$$= (1 - \beta_1)\lambda \left(\frac{P_{11}{}^2 EP_{21}}{I_{21}} + \frac{E^2 P_{21}{}^2 P_{11}}{I_{11}} \right)$$

113

the sign of which depends upon the signs of λ, P_{11}/I_{11}, and EP_{21}/I_{21}. Now the sign of P_{ij}/I_{ij} must clearly be the same as that of $P_{ij}I_{ij}$, which is easily found: From (126), (127), (155) and (157) it follows that

(166)
$$
\begin{aligned}
P_{11}I_{11} &= \frac{P_{11}X_{11}I_{11}}{X_{11}} = EP_{21}I_{21} = \frac{EP_{21}X_{21}I_{21}}{X_{21}} \\
&= (q_1 + q_2)\frac{W_1}{2} \frac{\{1 + \lambda(1 - c_1)[r_1 - (g_{F1} + g_{w1})]\}\beta_1{}^2}{\lambda[r_1 - (g_{F1} + g_{w1})]}
\end{aligned}
$$

Since q_1 and q_2 are both positive, (166) is positive if λ is. To see if λ is positive, insert (50), (51), and (117) into (119) and write the third first-order condition as

$$
\frac{\partial\phi_1}{\partial\lambda} = (1 - c_1)\beta_1 R_1 + (1 - c_1)W_1 - (P_{11}I_{11} + EP_{21}I_{21}) = 0
$$

Finally insert (166) and our collapsed-system solution (153), divide the *numéraire* W_1 away, rearrange, and solve the resulting equation for λ and find

(167)
$$
\lambda = \frac{\beta_1{}^2}{[\beta_1(1 - \beta_1) + 1/(q_1 + q_2)](1 - c_1)[r_1 - (g_{F1} + g_{w1})]}
$$

Assumptions already made ensure that all factors appearing on the right-hand side of (167) are positive, hence λ is positive, and the Hessian (165) is positive.

From the Hessian (165) remove the second column and the second row and obtain the bordered 2×2 principal minor

$$
\begin{vmatrix}
\dfrac{\partial^2\phi}{\partial I_{11}{}^2} & -P_{11} \\[2mm]
-P_{11} & 0
\end{vmatrix} = -P_{11}{}^2
$$

which is negative. Thus our collapsed system satisfies the second-order conditions for a maximum of Eq. (119).

Notes

[1] Borts, G. H., "A Theory of Long-Run International Capital Movements," *Jour. Pol. Econ.*, Aug. 1964, **72**, 341–359.

[2] Borts, G. H., and J. L. Stein, *Economic Growth in a Free Market*, New York, 1964.

[3] Graham, F. D., "The Theory of International Values Re-Examined," *Quart. Jour. Econ.*, Nov. 1923, **38**, 54–86.

[4] Hamada, K., "Economic Growth and Long-Term International Capital Movements," *Yale Econ. Essays*, Spring 1966, **6**, 49–96.

[5] Lund, H., *Svenska företags investeringar i utlandet*, Stockholm, 1967.

[6] Nelson, E. L., and F. Cutler, "The International Investment Position of the United States in 1967," *Surv. Curr. Bus.*, Oct. 1968, **48**, 19–32.

[7] Pizer, S., and F. Cutler, "Exports to Foreign Affiliates of U.S. Firms," *Surv. Curr. Bus.*, Dec. 1965, **45**, 13.

[8] Solow, R. M., "A Contribution to the Theory of Economic Growth," *Quart. Jour. Econ.*, Feb. 1956, **70**, 65–94.

[9] Deutsche Bundesbank, "Kapitalverkehr mit dem Ausland," *Monatsberichte der deutschen Bundesbank*, Apr. 1969, **21**, 64*.

8

Steady-State Unbalanced National Growth: Full Resource Allocation

With few exceptions, modern growth models are models of steady-state and balanced[a] growth of homogeneous consumption and capital stock, hence miss imbalance [1], [6] as well as most of what economics is supposedly all about: the allocation of resources.

The time has now come to take the third and final step towards a full-fledged allocation model. We shall take that step by abandoning the international economy studied in Chapters 6 and 7 and returning to a national one. Within a national economy, labor and capital are free to move among industries. A national economy, then, permits us to formulate the full problem of allocating labor, capital, and goods.

To allow for imbalance, a growth model needs at least two goods. But to formulate the full allocation problem, it will not do to let the two goods be the consumers' good and the producers' good found in Ricardo, Marx, and the usual [5] two-sector growth models. With only one consumer's good, such models are still models of homogeneous consumption, permitting no substitution among consumers' goods and asking no question, hence offering no answer, concerning the allocation of consumption expenditure among consumers' goods. With only one producers' good such models are still models of homogeneous capital stock, permitting no substitution among producers' goods and asking no question, hence offering no answer, concerning the allocation of investment expenditure among producers' goods.

We wish to build the simplest possible growth model of heterogeneous consumption as well as capital stock, thus allowing for the full allocation of resources. To do that we assume *each* of our two goods to serve interchangeably as a consumers' or as a producers' good: The physical output of the jth good is X_j where $j = 1, 2$. The jth good is produced from labor L_j and two immortal capital stocks S_{ij} where $i = 1, 2$. There are, then, four capital stocks S_{ij} and four investments I_{ij} in our model. Between two such industries we specify a fourfold interaction:

---

[a] We define, as Hahn and Matthews [3] did, steady-state growth as stationary proportionate rates of growth of physical outputs. We define, as Solow and Samuelson [4] did, balanced growth as identical proportionate rates of growth of physical output for all goods.

The two industries compete in their demand for labor. In the labor market they must pay the same money wage rate w, a parameter. Goods prices P_j are variables, hence the real wage rate w/P_j is also a variable.

The two industries compete in their demand for investment goods. In the market for the jth good they must pay the same price P_j. A firm producing the jth good and setting aside part of its own output for investment I_{jj} should charge itself the price P_j as an opportunity cost.

The two industries compete in their demand for money capital. In the money-capital market the capitalist-entrepreneurs allocate their savings between the two industries such as to maximize the present worth of all their future profits.

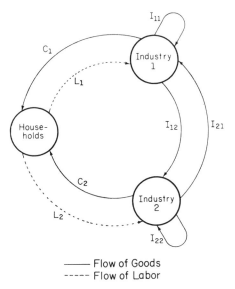

—— Flow of Goods
----- Flow of Labor

Figure 8-1. Physical flows.

The two industries compete in their supply of consumers' goods. In the consumers' goods market the two goods are good, but not perfect, substitutes, and each consumer has a taste for both of them.

Figure 8-1 shows all physical flows in our model. Section I defines variables and parameters. Section II specifies the model mathematically. Section III finds the equilibrium solutions for proportionate rates of growth. Section IV finds the equilibrium solutions for levels of variables. Certain proofs are banished to two appendices.

I. Notation

Variables

$C \equiv$ consumption

$\phi \equiv$ function to be maximized by the Lagrange-multiplier method

$g_v \equiv$ proportionate rate of growth of variable v where $v \equiv C, I, L, P, S, X,$ and Y

$I_{ij} \equiv$ investment of output of ith industry in jth industry

$\kappa_{ij} \equiv$ physical marginal productivity of capital stock S_{ij}

$L \equiv$ labor employed

$P \equiv$ price of good

$S_{ij} \equiv j$th industry's physical capital stock of ith industry's good

$U \equiv$ utility

$W \equiv$ wage bill

$X \equiv$ physical output

$Y \equiv$ national money income

$Z \equiv$ profits bill

$\zeta \equiv$ present worth of all future profits bills

Parameters

$A \equiv$ exponent of individual utility function

$\alpha, \beta \equiv$ exponents of production function

$c \equiv$ propensity to consume national money income

$F \equiv$ available labor force

$g_p \equiv$ proportionate rate of growth of parameter p where $p \equiv F, M,$ and w

$\lambda \equiv$ Lagrange multiplier

$M \equiv$ multiplicative factor of production function

$N \equiv$ multiplicative factor of individual utility function

$r \equiv$ discount rate applied by capitalist-entrepreneurs

$w \equiv$ money wage rate

Subscripts $i = 1, 2$ and $j = 1, 2$ refer to industry number.

All flow variables refer to the instantaneous rate of that variable measured on a per annum basis. The parameters listed are stationary except F, M, and w, whose proportionate rates of growth are stationary. Symbols t and τ are time coordinates. The symbol e is Euler's number, the base of natural logarithms. Symbols h, m, n, μ, v, ξ, π, ρ, and ψ stand for agglomerations of variables and parameters and will be defined as we go along.

II. The Equations of the Model

In Section I, 17 variable growth rates are listed, i.e., two growth rates of each of C_i, L_i, P_i, and X_i; four growth rates of each of I_{ij} and S_{ij}; and one growth rate of Y. To all apply the definition

(1) through (17)
$$g_v \equiv \frac{dv}{dt} \frac{1}{v}$$

Define investment as the derivative of capital stock with respect to time

(18) through (21)
$$I_{ij} \equiv \frac{dS_{ij}}{dt}$$

Let the jth industry apply the Cobb-Douglas production function

(22)
$$X_1 = M_1 L_1{}^{\alpha_1} S_{11}{}^{\beta_{11}} S_{21}{}^{\beta_{21}}$$

(23)
$$X_2 = M_2 L_2{}^{\alpha_2} S_{12}{}^{\beta_{12}} S_{22}{}^{\beta_{22}}$$

where $0 < \alpha_j < 1$; $0 < \beta_{ij} < 1$; $\alpha_1 + \beta_{11} + \beta_{21} = 1$; $\alpha_2 + \beta_{12} + \beta_{22} = 1$; and $M_j > 0$. In each industry let profit maximization under pure competition equalize real wage rate and physical marginal productivity of labor:

(24), (25)
$$\frac{w}{P_j} = \frac{\partial X_j}{\partial L_j} = \alpha_j \frac{X_j}{L_j}$$

Physical marginal productivities of capital at time t are

(26) through (29)
$$\kappa_{ij}(t) \equiv \frac{\partial X_j(t)}{\partial S_{ij}(t)} = \beta_{ij} \frac{X_j(t)}{S_{ij}(t)}$$

Multiply (26) through (29) by price of output of jth industry $P_j(t)$ to find value marginal productivities of capital at time t. Define money profits earned at time t on each physical unit of capital stock $S_{ij}(t)$ as its value marginal productivity. Then multiply by $S_{ij}(t)$ to find money profits earned at time t on capital stock $S_{ij}(t)$. Sum over $i = 1, 2$ and define the outcome as money profits earned at time t on whatever capital stock exists at that time in the entire jth industry:

(30), (31)
$$Z_j(t) \equiv \sum_{i=1}^{2} \kappa_{ij}(t) P_j(t) S_{ij}(t) = P_j(t) X_j(t) \sum_{i=1}^{2} \beta_{ij}$$

Sum over $j = 1, 2$ and define the outcome as money profits earned at time t on whatever capital stock exists at that time in the entire economy:

$$(32) \qquad Z(t) \equiv \sum_{j=1}^{2} Z_j(t)$$

As seen from the present time τ this profits bill is $Z(t)e^{-r(t-\tau)}$ where e is Euler's number, the base of natural logarithms, and r is the discount rate applied by the capitalist-entrepreneurs. Finally integrate this over $t = \tau$ through ∞ and define the outcome as the present worth of all future profits bills

$$(33) \qquad \zeta(\tau) \equiv \int_{\tau}^{\infty} Z(t)e^{-r(t-\tau)}\, dt$$

Now let capitalist-entrepreneurs use their control variable I_{ij} to optimize the allocation of their capital stock S_{ij} within as well as between industries. Within the jth industry they act as stockholders optimizing S_{ij} where $i = 1, 2$ by appointing the right managers. Between industries they act as stockholders optimizing S_{ij} where $j = 1, 2$ by purchasing stock in the right industry. "Optimizing" in what sense? In the sense that

$$(34) \qquad \zeta(\tau) = \text{maximum}$$

Under full employment, available labor force must equal the sum of labor employed by the two industries:

$$(35) \qquad F = \sum_{i=1}^{2} L_i$$

Define the wage bill as the money wage rate *times* employment:

$$(36) \qquad W \equiv w \sum_{i=1}^{2} L_i$$

Define national money income as the sum of the wage bill and the profits bill:

$$(37) \qquad Y \equiv W + Z$$

Let all persons have the same utility function. Let the utility function of the kth person be

$$U_k = N C_{1k}{}^{A_1} C_{2k}{}^{A_2}$$

where $0 < A_i < 1$ and $N > 0$. Let there be s persons, and let the kth person's money income be Y_k where

$$\sum_{k=1}^{s} Y_k = Y$$

Let all persons spend the fraction c, where $0 < c < 1$, of their money income. Then the budget constraint of the kth person is

$$cY_k = P_1 C_{1k} + P_2 C_{2k}$$

Maximize the kth person's utility subject to his budget constraint and find his two demand functions. Then add the s individual demand functions for each good and find the two Graham [2] aggregate demand functions

(38), (39)
$$C_i = \frac{\pi_i Y}{P_i}$$

where

$$\pi_i = \frac{cA_i}{A_1 + A_2}$$

Industry output equilibrium requires the output of the ith industry to equal the sum of consumption and investment demand for it, or inventory would either accumulate or be depleted:

(40), (41)
$$X_i = C_i + \sum_{j=1}^{2} I_{ij}$$

III. Solutions for Proportionate Rates of Growth

Our system (1) through (41) possesses the following set of steady-state solutions for its 17 equilibrium proportionate rates of growth:

(42), (43) $\quad g_{Ci} = g_{Xi}$

(44) through (47) $\quad g_{Iij} = g_{Xi}$

(48), (49) $\quad g_{Li} = g_F$

(50) $\quad g_{P1} = g_w - \dfrac{(1 - \beta_{22})g_{M1} + \beta_{21}g_{M2}}{(1 - \beta_{11})(1 - \beta_{22}) - \beta_{12}\beta_{21}}$

(51) $\quad g_{P2} = g_w - \dfrac{(1 - \beta_{11})g_{M2} + \beta_{12}g_{M1}}{(1 - \beta_{11})(1 - \beta_{22}) - \beta_{12}\beta_{21}}$

(52) through (55) $\quad g_{Sij} = g_{Xi}$

$$(56) \qquad g_{X1} = \frac{(1 - \beta_{22})g_{M1} + \beta_{21}g_{M2}}{(1 - \beta_{11})(1 - \beta_{22}) - \beta_{12}\beta_{21}} + g_F$$

$$(57) \qquad g_{X2} = \frac{(1 - \beta_{11})g_{M2} + \beta_{12}g_{M1}}{(1 - \beta_{11})(1 - \beta_{22}) - \beta_{12}\beta_{21}} + g_F$$

$$(58) \qquad g_Y = g_F + g_w$$

To see that it does, the reader should take derivatives with respect to time of all equations (18) through (41) except (26) through (29) and (33), (34). He should then use definitions (1) through (17), insert solutions (42) through (58), and convince himself that each equation is satisfied.

We defined balanced growth as identical proportionate rates of growth of physical output for all goods. According to our solutions (42) through (58), is our steady-state growth balanced or unbalanced?

Growth does spill over from one industry to the other. For example, according to (44) through (47) a more rapidly growing industry i would transmit some of its growth to a more slowly growing industry j investing in the ith industry's good. But the spillover is normally not enough to generate balanced growth. Use (56), (57), and the assumptions that $\alpha_1 + \beta_{11} + \beta_{21} = 1$ and $\alpha_2 + \beta_{12} + \beta_{22} = 1$ to find that

$$g_{X1} \gtreqless g_{X2} \qquad \text{implies} \qquad \frac{g_{M1}}{g_{M2}} \gtreqless \frac{\alpha_1}{\alpha_2}$$

respectively. Or in English: The first industry's physical output may grow more rapidly than that of the second industry for two and only[b] two reasons, i.e., first if everything else being equal the first industry has more rapid technological progress g_{Mi} than the second industry, second, if everything else being equal the physical output of the first industry has a lower labor elasticity α_i than that of the second industry: The less labor-sensitive industry is less hampered by the fact that under technological progress labor force is growing less rapidly than physical capital stocks.

It does, however, follow from (50), (51), (56), and (57) that unlike physical outputs X_i, industry revenues P_iX_i will grow at the same proportionate rate $g_F + g_w$.

---

[b] Our Graham-type demand functions (38) and (39) have unitary income elasticities. In our model, then, possible growth imbalance must have causes other than nonunitary income elasticities. From Yotopoulos-Lau [6] one may conclude that nonunitary sector income elasticities play a minuscule role in explaining real-world growth imbalance. This conclusion is derived in Appendix III.

IV. Solutions for Levels

So much for proportionate rates of growth. Let us now turn to the allocation of resources and solve for the allocation of savings between industries; the levels of industry revenues; employments; national money income; physical outputs; prices; physical capital stocks and their physical marginal productivities; consumption; and income distribution.

1. Saving Equals Investment

Use (24), (25), and (36) to see that $W = \alpha_1 P_1 X_1 + \alpha_2 P_2 X_2$, and (30) through (32) to see that $Z = (\beta_{11} + \beta_{21})P_1 X_1 + (\beta_{12} + \beta_{22})P_2 X_2$, hence national income equals national output:

$$(59) \qquad Y = P_1 X_1 + P_2 X_2$$

Multiply (40) and (41) by P_1 and P_2, respectively, insert (38), (39), and (59) and find saving to equal investment:

$$(60) \qquad (1 - c)Y = P_1(I_{11} + I_{12}) + P_2(I_{21} + I_{22})$$

2. Present-Worth Maximization

Subject to the constraint (60) let the capitalist-entrepreneurs use their control variable I_{ij} to optimize the allocation of their capital stock S_{ij} within as well as between industries. "Optimize" in what sense? In the sense of maximizing the present worth $\zeta(\tau)$ of all future profits bills in accordance with (34). Using (30) through (33) we write present worth as

$$\zeta(\tau) = \int_\tau^\infty [(\beta_{11} + \beta_{21})P_1(t)X_1(t) + (\beta_{12} + \beta_{22})P_2(t)X_2(t)]e^{-r(t-\tau)}\, dt$$

Let it be foreseen by the capitalist-entrepreneurs that prices are growing in accordance with our steady-state solutions (50) and (51), hence

$$P_j(t) = e^{g_{Pj}(t-\tau)}P_j(\tau)$$

and that outputs are growing in accordance with our steady-state solutions (56) and (57), hence

$$X_j(t) = e^{g_{Xj}(t-\tau)}X_j(\tau)$$

Consequently we may take prices and outputs outside the integral sign and write present worth as

$$\zeta(\tau) = (\beta_{11} + \beta_{21})P_1(\tau)X_1(\tau)\int_\tau^\infty e^{(g_{P1} + g_{X1} - r)(t-\tau)}\,dt$$

$$+ (\beta_{12} + \beta_{22})P_2(\tau)X_2(\tau)\int_\tau^\infty e^{(g_{P2} + g_{X2} - r)(t-\tau)}\,dt$$

Since in this expression all variables refer to the same time τ, we may purge it of τ. Use (50), (51), (56), and (57) to see that $g_{Pj} + g_{Xj} = g_F + g_w$. Assume that $g_F + g_w < r$, then integrate:

$$\zeta = \frac{(\beta_{11} + \beta_{21})P_1X_1 + (\beta_{12} + \beta_{22})P_2X_2}{r - (g_F + g_w)}$$

Inserting (30) through (32) into this we find the simple relationship between profits and present worth under steady-state growth:

(61) $$Z = [r - (g_F + g_w)]\zeta$$

Maximizing present worth ζ subject to the constraint (60) is most easily done by using a Lagrange multiplier: Define a new function to be maximized

$$\phi \equiv \zeta + \lambda[(1 - c)Y - P_1(I_{11} + I_{12}) - P_2(I_{21} + I_{22})]$$

What to do with Y? Insert (61) into (37), insert the outcome into ϕ and write the latter

(62) $$\phi = \{1 + \lambda(1 - c)[r - (g_F + g_w)]\}\zeta$$
$$+ \lambda(1 - c)W - \lambda[P_1(I_{11} + I_{12}) + P_2(I_{21} + I_{22})]$$

The first four first-order conditions for a maximum ϕ are

(63) $$\frac{\partial\phi}{\partial I_{ij}} = h_j\frac{\partial X_j}{\partial I_{ij}} - \lambda P_i = 0$$

where

$$h_j \equiv \frac{\{1 + \lambda(1 - c)[r - (g_F + g_w)]\}(\beta_{1j} + \beta_{2j})P_j}{r - (g_F + g_w)}$$

Now according to the production functions (22) and (23), output X_j is a function of capital stock S_{ij} rather than of investment I_{ij}. But according to (1) through (21)

(64) $$S_{ij} \equiv \frac{I_{ij}}{g_{Sij}}$$

where our steady-state growth, as specified by (52) through (57), permits us to express g_{Sij} solely in terms of parameters. Inserting (64) into the production functions (22) and (23) we find

$$(65) \qquad \frac{\partial X_j}{\partial I_{ij}} = \beta_{ij} \frac{X_j}{I_{ij}}$$

and write the first-order conditions as

$$(66) \text{ through } (69) \quad \frac{\beta_{11}(\beta_{11} + \beta_{21})X_1}{I_{11}} = \frac{\beta_{12}(\beta_{12} + \beta_{22})P_2 X_2}{P_1 I_{12}}$$

$$= \frac{\beta_{21}(\beta_{11} + \beta_{21})P_1 X_1}{P_2 I_{21}}$$

$$= \frac{\beta_{22}(\beta_{12} + \beta_{22})X_2}{I_{22}}$$

$$= \frac{\lambda[r - (g_F + g_w)]}{1 + \lambda(1 - c)[r - (g_F + g_w)]}$$

That the second-order conditions are satisfied is demonstrated in Appendix I.

3. Solving for Industry Revenues $P_j X_j$

Use the first-order conditions (66) through (68) to express I_{12} in terms of I_{11} and I_{21} in terms of I_{22}. Insert the results into (40) and (41). Insert (59) into (38) and (39). Insert the results into (40) and (41). Divide (40) by $\beta_{11}(\beta_{11} + \beta_{21})X_1$ and (41) by $\beta_{22}(\beta_{12} + \beta_{22})X_2$, deduct (41) from (40), and again use the first-order conditions (66) through (68). Now define

$$(70) \qquad \rho \equiv \frac{P_1 X_1}{P_2 X_2}$$

rearrange, and write the quadratic

$$(71) \qquad \rho^2 + m\rho + n = 0$$

where m and n are the following agglomerations of taste and technology parameters

$$m \equiv \frac{(\beta_{12} + \beta_{22})[\beta_{12}\pi_2 + \beta_{22}(1 - \pi_1)] - (\beta_{11} + \beta_{21})[\beta_{11}(1 - \pi_2) + \beta_{21}\pi_1]}{(\beta_{11} + \beta_{21})[\beta_{11}\pi_2 + \beta_{21}(1 - \pi_1)]}$$

$$n \equiv -\frac{(\beta_{12} + \beta_{22})[\beta_{12}(1 - \pi_2) + \beta_{22}\pi_1]}{(\beta_{11} + \beta_{21})[\beta_{11}\pi_2 + \beta_{21}(1 - \pi_1)]}$$

The quadratic has the two roots

$$\rho = -\frac{m}{2} \pm \sqrt{\left(\frac{m}{2}\right)^2 - n}$$

We have assumed that $0 < A_i < 1$, $0 < \beta_i < 1$, and $0 < c < 1$, hence $n < 0$. Now regardless of the sign of m, $0 \le (m/2)^2$, hence

$$0 \le \left(\frac{m}{2}\right)^2 < \left(\frac{m}{2}\right)^2 - n$$

Two things follow. First, from $0 < (m/2)^2 - n$ it follows that both roots are real. Second, from $(m/2)^2 < (m/2)^2 - n$ it follows that regardless of the sign of m, the first root is positive and the second negative. We reject the latter and are left with

(72)
$$\rho = -\frac{m}{2} + \sqrt{\left(\frac{m}{2}\right)^2 - n}$$

Use (24), (25), (35), and (36) to find

$$\alpha_1 P_1 X_1 + \alpha_2 P_2 X_2 = wF$$

Take this together with (70) and find

(73), (74)
$$P_i X_i = \mu_i w F$$

where

$$\mu_1 \equiv \frac{\rho}{\alpha_1 \rho + \alpha_2}$$

$$\mu_2 \equiv \frac{1}{\alpha_1 \rho + \alpha_2}$$

4. Solving for Employments L_i and Income Y

Use (24), (25), (73), (74) to solve for employments

(75), (76)
$$L_i = \alpha_i \mu_i F$$

Insert (73) and (74) into (59) and solve for national money income

(77)
$$Y = (\mu_1 + \mu_2) w F$$

5. Solving for Physical Outputs X_j

Let us begin by finding four investment-output ratios. Again use the first-order conditions (66) through (68) to express I_{12} in terms of I_{11}. Insert the result into (40), insert (59) into (38), and insert the result into (40). Divide (40) by X_1. Use a similar procedure upon (41) and find the four ratios

$$(78) \qquad \frac{I_{11}}{X_1} = v_{11} \equiv \frac{1 - \pi_1 - \pi_1/\rho}{1 + \beta_{12}(\beta_{12} + \beta_{22})/[\rho\beta_{11}(\beta_{11} + \beta_{21})]}$$

$$(79) \qquad \frac{I_{12}}{X_1} = v_{12} \equiv \frac{1 - \pi_1 - \pi_1/\rho}{1 + \rho\beta_{11}(\beta_{11} + \beta_{21})/[\beta_{12}(\beta_{12} + \beta_{22})]}$$

$$(80) \qquad \frac{I_{21}}{X_2} = v_{21} \equiv \frac{1 - \pi_2 - \pi_2\rho}{1 + \beta_{22}(\beta_{12} + \beta_{22})/[\rho\beta_{21}(\beta_{11} + \beta_{21})]}$$

$$(81) \qquad \frac{I_{22}}{X_2} = v_{22} \equiv \frac{1 - \pi_2 - \pi_2\rho}{1 + \rho\beta_{21}(\beta_{11} + \beta_{21})/[\beta_{22}(\beta_{12} + \beta_{22})]}$$

Apply (64) to (78) through (81) and find

$$(82) \qquad S_{ij} = \frac{X_i v_{ij}}{g_{sij}}$$

Insert (82) and our solutions (75) and (76) into the production functions (22) and (23), arrive at two equations in the two unknowns X_j, solve them, and find

$$(83) \qquad X_1 = (\xi_1^{\,1-\beta_{22}}\xi_2^{\,\beta_{21}})^{1/[(1-\beta_{11})(1-\beta_{22})-\beta_{12}\beta_{21}]}F$$

$$(84) \qquad X_2 = (\xi_1^{\,\beta_{12}}\xi_2^{\,1-\beta_{11}})^{1/[(1-\beta_{11})(1-\beta_{22})-\beta_{12}\beta_{21}]}F$$

where

$$\xi_1 \equiv M_1(\alpha_1\mu_1)^{\alpha_1}\left(\frac{v_{11}}{g_{s11}}\right)^{\beta_{11}}\left(\frac{v_{21}}{g_{s21}}\right)^{\beta_{21}}$$

$$\xi_2 \equiv M_2(\alpha_2\mu_2)^{\alpha_2}\left(\frac{v_{12}}{g_{s12}}\right)^{\beta_{12}}\left(\frac{v_{22}}{g_{s22}}\right)^{\beta_{22}}$$

The reader may convince himself that (83) and (84) are indeed growing at the rates (56) and (57) said they should be.

6. *Solving for Prices P_j*

Divide our revenue solutions (73) and (74) by our physical output solutions (83) and (84), respectively, and find

(85) $$P_1 = (\xi_1^{1-\beta_{22}}\xi_2^{\beta_{21}})^{-1/[(1-\beta_{11})(1-\beta_{22})-\beta_{12}\beta_{21}]}w\mu_1$$

(86) $$P_2 = (\xi_1^{\beta_{12}}\xi_2^{1-\beta_{11}})^{-1/[(1-\beta_{11})(1-\beta_{22})-\beta_{12}\beta_{21}]}w\mu_2$$

Similarly the reader may convince himself that (85) and (86) are indeed growing at the rates (50) and (51) said they should be.

7. *Capital Stocks S_{ij} and their Marginal Productivities κ_{ij}*

With (83) and (84) inserted into it (82) will be a solution for physical capital stocks S_{ij}. With (82) through (84) inserted into them, (26) through (29) will be solutions for the physical marginal productivities of capital. Notice that the numerator and denominator of (26) through (29) are X_j and S_{ij}, respectively, and that according to (52) through (55) $g_{Sij} = g_{Xi}$. Consequently, in κ_{ii} numerator and denominator are growing at the same proportionate rate, hence κ_{ii} is stationary. Indeed, write (82) for $j = i$, insert it into (26) through (29), and find

(87) $$\kappa_{ii} = \frac{\beta_{ii}g_{Sii}}{v_{ii}}$$

But in κ_{ij} where $i \neq j$ numerator and denominator are not growing at the same proportionate rate. If $g_{M1}/g_{M2} > \alpha_1/\alpha_2$, growth is unbalanced: $g_{X1} > g_{X2}$ and κ_{12} is decaying and κ_{21} growing. Vice versa if $g_{M1}/g_{M2} < \alpha_1/\alpha_2$.

8. *Consumption C_i and Income Distribution W and Z*

With (77), (85), and (86) inserted into them, (38) and (39) will be solutions for consumption. Insert (35) into (36) and find the wage bill

(88) $$W = wF$$

Insert (73) and (74) into (30) through (32) and find the profits bill

(89) $$Z = [(\beta_{11} + \beta_{21})\mu_1 + (\beta_{12} + \beta_{22})\mu_2]wF$$

With (89) inserted into it, (61) is a solution for present worth.

9. *Properties of Solutions*

We have solved for the levels of all variables. Our solutions (78) through (81) for the investment-output ratios and (87) for two of the four physical marginal productivities of capital are stationary. All other solutions for levels are nonstationary, because they contain one or more of our three nonstationary parameters, i.e., available labor force F, the multiplicative factor M_i of the production functions, and the money wage rate w.

Are our solutions real and positive? Section IV, 3 found both roots ρ to be real and found one to be positive, the other negative. All solutions (73) through (89), then, are real. Rejecting the negative root we find solutions (73) through (77), (88), and (89) to be obviously positive. Less obviously, so are solutions (78) through (87), as demonstrated in our Appendix II.

Write the bordered Hessian

$$(90) \quad H \equiv \begin{vmatrix} \dfrac{\partial^2 \phi}{\partial I_{11}{}^2} & \dfrac{\partial^2 \phi}{\partial I_{11}\partial I_{12}} & \dfrac{\partial^2 \phi}{\partial I_{11}\partial I_{21}} & \dfrac{\partial^2 \phi}{\partial I_{11}\partial I_{22}} & -P_1 \\[2mm] \dfrac{\partial^2 \phi}{\partial I_{12}\partial I_{11}} & \dfrac{\partial^2 \phi}{\partial I_{12}{}^2} & \dfrac{\partial^2 \phi}{\partial I_{12}\partial I_{21}} & \dfrac{\partial^2 \phi}{\partial I_{12}\partial I_{22}} & -P_1 \\[2mm] \dfrac{\partial^2 \phi}{\partial I_{21}\partial I_{11}} & \dfrac{\partial^2 \phi}{\partial I_{21}\partial I_{12}} & \dfrac{\partial^2 \phi}{\partial I_{21}{}^2} & \dfrac{\partial^2 \phi}{\partial I_{21}\partial I_{22}} & -P_2 \\[2mm] \dfrac{\partial^2 \phi}{\partial I_{22}\partial I_{11}} & \dfrac{\partial^2 \phi}{\partial I_{22}\partial I_{12}} & \dfrac{\partial^2 \phi}{\partial I_{22}\partial I_{21}} & \dfrac{\partial^2 \phi}{\partial I_{22}{}^2} & -P_2 \\[2mm] -P_1 & -P_1 & -P_2 & -P_2 & 0 \end{vmatrix}$$

The first derivatives $\partial\phi/\partial I_{ij}$ have already been taken and were of the form (63). It follows from that form that a good many of the second derivatives contained in our Hessian are zero: After inserting (64) into our production functions (22) and (23) we realize that X_j is a function of neither I_{ii} nor I_{ji} where $i \neq j$, hence

$$(91) \quad \frac{\partial X_j}{\partial I_{ii}} = \frac{\partial X_j}{\partial I_{ji}} = \frac{\partial^2 X_j}{\partial I_{ii}\partial I_{ij}} = \frac{\partial^2 X_j}{\partial I_{ji}\partial I_{ij}} = \frac{\partial^2 X_j}{\partial I_{ii}\partial I_{jj}} = \frac{\partial^2 X_j}{\partial I_{ji}\partial I_{jj}} = 0$$
$$(i \neq j)$$

But X_j is a function of I_{ij} and I_{jj}, hence

$$(92) \quad \frac{\partial^2 X_j}{\partial I_{ij}\partial I_{jj}} = \frac{\partial^2 X_j}{\partial I_{jj}\partial I_{ij}} = \frac{\beta_{ij}\beta_{jj}X_j}{I_{ij}I_{jj}} \quad (i \neq j)$$

$$(93) \quad \frac{\partial^2 X_j}{\partial I_{ij}{}^2} = \beta_{ij}(\beta_{ij} - 1)\frac{X_j}{I_{ij}{}^2} \quad (i = j \quad \text{or} \quad i \neq j)$$

Apply (91), (92), and (93) to the Hessian (90). Then try to produce even more zero elements, making the Hessian easier to evaluate. Factor out $\beta_{11}h_1X_1/I_{11}$ from first row; $\beta_{12}h_2X_2/I_{12}$ from second row; $\beta_{21}h_1X_1/I_{21}$

131

from third row; and $\beta_{22}h_2X_2/I_{22}$ from fourth row, where h was defined as part of (63). Thereby the first four elements of the fifth column become

$$-\frac{P_1I_{11}}{\beta_{11}h_1X_1}$$

$$-\frac{P_1I_{12}}{\beta_{12}h_2X_2}$$

$$-\frac{P_2I_{21}}{\beta_{21}h_1X_1}$$

$$-\frac{P_2I_{22}}{\beta_{22}h_2X_2}$$

But according to the first-order conditions (66) through (69) those four values are all equal to $-1/\lambda$. Now factor out $1/I_{11}$ from first column, $1/I_{12}$ from second column, $1/I_{21}$ from third column, $1/I_{22}$ from fourth column, and $1/\lambda$ from fifth column.

If to each element of a row is added the corresponding element of another row, the determinant remains unchanged. So factor out (-1) from the first row and add to each element of it the corresponding element of the third row. Factor out (-1) from the second row and add to each element of it the corresponding element of the fourth row.

If to each element of a column is added the corresponding element of another column, the determinant remains unchanged. So add to each element of the third column the corresponding element of the first column. Add to each element of the fourth column the corresponding element of the second column.

By now the Hessian has been transformed into the following very tractable form:

$$H = \frac{\beta_{11}\beta_{12}\beta_{21}\beta_{22}h_1^2h_2^2X_1^2X_2^2}{I_{11}^2I_{12}^2I_{21}^2I_{22}^2\lambda}$$

$$\times \begin{vmatrix} 1 & 0 & 0 & 0 & 0 \\ 0 & 1 & 0 & 0 & 0 \\ \beta_{11} & 0 & -\alpha_1 & 0 & -1 \\ 0 & \beta_{12} & 0 & -\alpha_2 & -1 \\ -P_1I_{11} & -P_1I_{12} & -P_1I_{11} - P_2I_{21} & -P_1I_{12} - P_2I_{22} & 0 \end{vmatrix}$$

$$= \frac{\beta_{11}\beta_{12}\beta_{21}\beta_{22}h_1^2h_2^2X_1^2X_2^2}{I_{11}^2I_{12}^2I_{21}^2I_{22}^2\lambda}\left[\alpha_2(P_1I_{11} + P_2I_{21}) + \alpha_1(P_1I_{12} + P_2I_{22})\right]$$

Is our Hessian positive, then? Appendix II will demonstrate that all solutions, including those for $P_i I_{ij}$, are positive. To see if λ is positive, write the fifth first-order condition $\partial \phi / \partial \lambda = 0$ and find it to be the constraint (60). Use (66) through (69) to write

$$P_1(I_{11} + I_{12}) + P_2(I_{21} + I_{22}) = \frac{1 + \lambda(1 - c)[r - (g_F + g_w)]}{\lambda[r - (g_F + g_w)]}$$

$$\times \left[(\beta_{11} + \beta_{21})^2 P_1 X_1 + (\beta_{12} + \beta_{22})^2 P_2 X_2\right]$$

Insert (59) and this into the constraint (60), rearrange, and write the latter

$$\lambda = \frac{\psi}{(1 - c)(1 - \psi)[r - (g_F + g_w)]}$$

where

$$\psi \equiv \frac{(\beta_{11} + \beta_{21})^2 P_1 X_1 + (\beta_{12} + \beta_{22})^2 P_2 X_2}{P_1 X_1 + P_2 X_2}$$

It follows from $0 < \psi < 1$ that $\lambda > 0$, hence the Hessian (90) is positive. And now for its principal minors.

From the Hessian (90) remove successively fourth, third, and second column and row and obtain the bordered 4×4, 3×3, and 2×2 principal minors. Their values are respectively

$$-\frac{\beta_{11}\beta_{12}\beta_{21}h_1{}^2 h_2 X_1{}^2 X_2}{I_{11}{}^2 I_{12}{}^2 I_{21}{}^2 \lambda} \left[(1 - \beta_{12})(P_1 I_{11} + P_2 I_{21})\right.$$

$$\left. + (1 - \beta_{11} - \beta_{21})P_1 I_{12}\right]$$

$$\frac{\beta_{11}\beta_{12}h_1 h_2 X_1 X_2}{I_{11}{}^2 I_{12}{}^2 \lambda} \left[(1 - \beta_{12})P_1 I_{11} + (1 - \beta_{11})P_1 I_{12}\right]$$

$$-\frac{\beta_{11}h_1 X_1}{I_{11}{}^2 \lambda} P_1 I_{11}$$

The three values are negative, positive, and negative, respectively.

Solutions (78) through (87) contain one of the factors v_{ij}. Could those factors be nonpositive? To show that they cannot we prove that our positive root ρ has the following bounds:

$$(94) \qquad \frac{\pi_1}{1 - \pi_1} < \rho < \frac{1 - \pi_2}{\pi_2}$$

Take the first inequality of (94), insert (72), move the term $-(m/2)$ to the other side, and write the inequality

$$(95) \qquad \sqrt{\left(\frac{m}{2}\right)^2 - n} > \frac{m}{2} + \frac{\pi_1}{1 - \pi_1}$$

Square the inequality, multiply it by $(1 - \pi_1)^2$, and write it

$$(96) \qquad -\pi_1^2 - m\pi_1(1 - \pi_1) - n(1 - \pi_1)^2 > 0$$

Now insert the definitions of m and n attached to (71), multiply on both sides by their positive common denominator, recall that $\pi_1 + \pi_2 = c$, rearrange, and find

$$(97) \qquad (1 - c)[(\beta_{11} + \beta_{21})\beta_{11}\pi_1 + (\beta_{12} + \beta_{22})\beta_{12}(1 - \pi_1)] > 0$$

which is true under our assumptions about β_{ij} and π_i.

Could we have done all this in reverse order, deriving the first inequality of (94) from (97)? Eq. (95) would then have been the two inequalities

$$\pm\sqrt{\left(\frac{m}{2}\right)^2 - n} \gtrless \pm\left(\frac{m}{2} + \frac{\pi_1}{1 - \pi_1}\right)$$

of which, however, the former can be derived from the latter by multiplying the latter by -1 and reversing the inequality sign. So we could indeed have derived the first inequality of (94) from (97). Since (97) is known to be true, the first inequality of (94) must be!

Then take the second inequality of (94), insert (72), move the term $-(m/2)$ to the other side, and write the inequality as

$$(98) \qquad \sqrt{\left(\frac{m}{2}\right)^2 - n} < \frac{m}{2} + \frac{1 - \pi_2}{\pi_2}$$

Square the inequality, multiplying it by π_2^2, and write it

(99) $(1 - \pi_2)^2 + m\pi_2(1 - \pi_2) + n\pi_2^2 > 0$

Insert the definitions of m and n, multiply on both sides by their positive common denominator, recall that $\pi_1 + \pi_2 = c$, rearrange, and find

(100) $(1 - c)[(\beta_{11} + \beta_{21})\beta_{21}(1 - \pi_2) + (\beta_{12} + \beta_{22})\beta_{22}\pi_2] > 0$

which is true under our assumptions about β_{ij} and π_i.

Could we have done all this in reverse order, deriving the second inequality of (94) from (100)? Eq. (98) would then have been the two inequalities

$$\pm\sqrt{\left(\frac{m}{2}\right)^2 - n} \lessgtr \pm\left(\frac{m}{2} + \frac{1 - \pi_2}{\pi_2}\right)$$

of which, however, the former can be derived from the latter by multiplying the latter by -1 and reversing the inequality sign. So we could indeed have derived the second inequality of (94) from (100). Since (100) is known to be true, the second inequality of (94) must be!

Having validated (94), take its first inequality, multiply it by $1 - \pi_1$, divide it by ρ, use the definitions (78), (79), and find

$$v_{11} > 0 \qquad v_{12} > 0$$

Take the second inequality of (94), multiply it by π_2, use the definitions (80), (81), and find

$$v_{21} > 0 \qquad v_{22} > 0$$

We conclude that (78) through (87) are indeed positive: Both goods will be produced, consumed, and invested; both goods will have positive prices.

Appendix III: Empirical Measurement of Growth Imbalance

Yotopoulos and Lau [6] have examined growth imbalance in 65 countries for the periods 1948–53, 1954–58, and 1950–60. In each country, six sectors were distinguished, i.e., agriculture, mining, manufacturing, construction, electricity-gas-water, and "others", including transportation and communication, services, etc.

Modifying the Yotopoulos-Lau notation slightly to make it consistent with our own, let us define

E_i ≡ income elasticity of demand for output of ith sector
G ≡ proportionate rate of growth of gross domestic product in constant prices
g_{Xi} ≡ proportionate rate of growth of output of ith sector in constant prices
ω_i ≡ share in gross domestic product of value added by ith sector

Yotopoulos-Lau now applied two different concepts of imbalance. First, an index of Samuelson-Solow-von Neumann imbalance defined as

$$(101) \qquad V^* \equiv \frac{1}{G} \sqrt{\sum_{i=1}^{n} \omega_i (g_{Xi} - G)^2}$$

or, in English, the reciprocal of the national real growth rate *times* the square root of the weighted sum of the squared deviations of sectoral real growth rates from the national real growth rate.

For their entire sample of 65 countries, Yotopoulos-Lau found a rather strong negative correlation between the Samuelson-Solow-von Neumann index of imbalance and the national real growth rate; The coefficient of correlation was -0.322. They also found the most highly developed countries to have the lowest index of imbalance.

From the Yotopoulos-Lau sample of 65 countries, our own Figure 8-2 has selected, for the period 1950–60, a much smaller sample consisting of the 19 capitalist countries which had, in 1958, a per capita income of $500 or more per annum. Figure 8-2 shows that even those countries still had a substantial Samuelson-Solow-von Neumann index of imbalance: Their square root of the weighted sum of squared deviations ranged from 0.19 (Venezuela) to 1.26 (Uruguay) of the national real growth rate, with the majority of the countries lying between 0.30 and 0.55 of that rate.

137

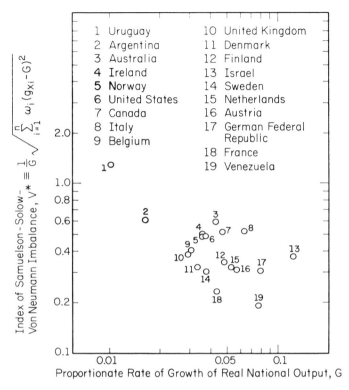

Figure 8-2. Samuelson-Solow-Von Neumann imbalance in 19 countries, 1950–1960.

Could imbalance be explained by nonunitary sector income elasticities? Here it occurred to Yotopoulos-Lau to define a second index of imbalance removing from the imbalance concept those deviations which are caused by nonunitary sector income elasticities. That index they called a Nurkse imbalance index and defined it as

(102) $$V' \equiv \frac{1}{G} \sqrt{\sum_{i=1}^{n} \omega_i (g_{Xi} - E_i G)^2}$$

or, in English, the reciprocal of the national real growth rate *times* the square root of the weighted sum of the squared deviations of sectoral real growth rates from the product of sector income elasticity and national real growth rate.

Now suppose that imbalance were fully explained by nonunitary sector income elasticities. Then the output of the *i*th sector would always be growing at the rate $g_{Xi} = E_i G$, consequently according to (102) $V' = 0$. In other words, Nurkse imbalance would be zero.

Applying to the same period and the same countries as Figure 8-2, our Figure 8-3 shows that Nurkse imbalance is far from zero. The Nurkse imbalance in Figure 8-3 is almost as substantial as the Samuelson-Solow-von Neumann imbalance in Figure 8-2. The Nurkse range has the same floor but a

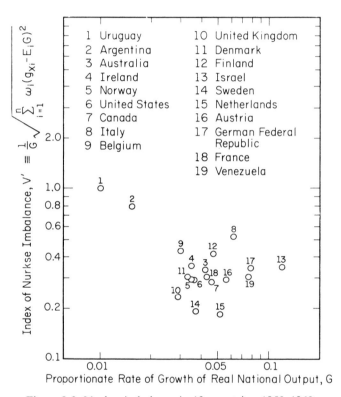

Figure 8-3. Nurkse imbalance in 19 countries, 1950–1960.

slightly lower ceiling than the Samuelson-Solow-von Neumann range: The square root of the weighted sum of squared Nurkse deviations ranges from 0.19 (the Netherlands) to 1.0 (Uruguay) of the national real growth rate, with a majority of the countries lying between 0.25 and 0.50 of that rate. We conclude that the Nurkse index has removed precious little imbalance from the Samuelson-Solow-von Neumann index.

How come, so little? Suppose all sector income elasticities were unity, then the Samuelson-Solow-von Neumann index would become equal to the Nurkse index: If $E_i = 1$ it follows from (101) and (102) that $V^* = V'$. And indeed the income elasticities used by Yotopoulos-Lau differed very little from unity:

Agriculture	0.952
Mining	0.892
Manufacturing	1.044
Construction	1.035
Electricity-gas-water	1.045
Others	0.999

These sector income elasticities were estimated from cross sections of some of the countries examined but applied to all countries.

From the Yotopoulos-Lau measurements we conclude three things. First, that growth imbalance is a rather ubiquitous phenomenon. Second, that in highly developed countries it is not strongly correlated with the national real growth rate. Third, that nonunitary sector income elasticities play a miniscule role in explaining real-world growth imbalance.

Notes

[1] Denison, E. F., *Why Growth Rates Differ*, Washington, D.C., 1967, Ch. 16.

[2] Graham, F. D., "The Theory of International Values Re-Examined," *Quart. J. Econ.*, Nov. 1923, **38,** 54–86.

[3] Hahn, F. H., and R. C. O. Matthews, "The Theory of Economic Growth: A Survey," *Econ. J.*, Dec. 1964, **74,** 779–902.

[4] Solow, R. M., and P. A. Samuelson, "Balanced Growth under Constant Returns to Scale," *Econometrica*, July 1953, **21,** 412–424.

[5] Uzawa, H., "On a Two-Sector Model of Economic Growth," I-II, *Rev. Econ. Stud.*, Oct. 1961, **29,** 40–47 and June 1963, **30,** 105–118.

[6] Yotopoulos, P. A., and L. J. Lau, "A Test for Balanced and Unbalanced Growth," *Rev. Econ. Stat.*, Nov. 1970, **52,** 376–384.

IV. Capital Quickening

Technological Progress and Optimal Replacement

Chapters 3 and 4 assumed technological progress to be absent, and Chapters 5 through 8 assumed it to be present only in disembodied form. But much technological progress makes its way into the economy in the form of new and physically different hardware—as Ricardo observed, cf. our Chapter 1, Section 5! How much? For the United States 1929–1958 Intriligator [1] found disembodied and embodied technological progress to be 0.017 and 0.04 per annum, respectively. Capital-embodied progress was found to be more important than labor-embodied progress. But using Australian data 1949/50–1959/60 Lydall [2] found disembodied technological progress to have been the more important form.

However this may be, we wish to come to grips with embodied technological progress: Assume that under steady technological progress no retired producers' good will be replaced by another physically identical to it. It will be replaced by a new and physically different one, and not until this happens can technological progress be exploited.

Exactly when should such replacement take place? Obviously not too soon, or the cost of acquiring new producers' goods occurs too frequently. But producers' goods should not be replaced too late either, or the falling price of their output catches up with them. Their efficiency remains stationary, while new and more efficient producers' goods of later vintages become available to the firm itself, its rivals, and to potential entrants to the industry.

We see a practically important form of labor-capital substitution here, i.e., the substitution between replacing and replaced producers' goods. At the margin of replacement the efficiency difference between replacing and replaced producers' goods may be considerable. For example, let technological progress amount to a 3 per cent efficiency increase per annum, and let useful life be 26 years—two empirically plausible figures. Then the replacing unit has a 2.18 times higher efficiency than the replaced one!

1. Notation

Variables

$C \equiv$ consumption
$H \equiv$ revenue *minus* operating labor cost per physical unit of producers' goods
$I \equiv$ investment
$J \equiv$ present net worth of an endless series of generations of producers' goods maintaining constant capacity
$k \equiv$ present gross worth of a physical unit of producers' goods
$L_1 \equiv$ labor employed by producers' goods industry
$L_2 \equiv$ labor employed by consumers' goods industry
$n \equiv$ present net worth of a physical unit of producers' goods
$P \equiv$ price of consumers' goods
$p \equiv$ price of producers' goods
$u \equiv$ useful life of producers' goods
$X \equiv$ physical output of consumers' goods

Parameters

$a \equiv$ labor required to produce one physical unit of producers' goods
$b \equiv$ physical capital coefficient
$\eta \equiv$ price elasticity of demand for consumers' goods
$N \equiv$ multiplicative factor in demand function for consumers' goods
$q \equiv$ proportionate rate of technological progress
$r \equiv$ rate of interest
$w \equiv$ money wage rate

All flow variables refer to the instantaneous rate of that variable measured on a per annum basis. The parameters listed are stationary except b, whose proportionate rate of growth q is stationary.

The symbol v is a vintage coordinate applied to capital coefficients b, labor employed by the consumers' goods industry L_2, and output of consumers' goods X. Symbol t is the time coordinate. The symbol e is Euler's number, the base of natural logarithms.

2. The Producers' Goods Industry

Let us borrow a leaf from Ricardo and assume the production function of the producers' goods industry to have only one input in it, i.e., labor. Let a be the labor required to produce one physical unit of producers' goods of any vintage, then

$$(1) \qquad\qquad L_1 = aI$$

where a is a technological parameter. Let there be pure competition and freedom of entry and exit in the producers' goods industry, then the price of producers' goods will equal their cost of production per unit:

$$(2) \qquad\qquad p = aw$$

3. The Consumers' Goods Industry

Let a firm in the consumers' goods industry be facing the demand function

$$(3) \qquad\qquad C = NP^{\eta}$$

where $\eta < -1$ and $N > 0$.

All producers' goods of the same vintage are physically identical. The physical capital coefficient $b(v)$ of producers' goods of vintage v is defined as their number divided by their output:

$$(4) \qquad\qquad b(v) \equiv \frac{I(v)}{X(v)}$$

Producers' goods of different vintages are not physically identical. Let technological progress manifest itself in a steady reduction of the physical capital coefficient such that

$$(5) \qquad\qquad b(t) = e^{q(t-v)}b(v)$$

where $q < 0$. But if producers' goods of different vintages are not physically identical, how do we define a physical unit of them? How do we compare spades and bulldozers? Simply define a physical unit of producers' goods as the equipment operated by one man. Then

$$(6) \qquad\qquad L_2(v) \equiv I(v)$$

Let there be a steady reduction of the price charged by the firm such that

$$(7) \qquad\qquad P(t) = e^{q(t-v)}P(v)$$

4. Net Worth of a New Physical Unit of Producers' Goods

Let the capital coefficient of a physical unit of producers' goods of vintage v be unchangeable for the entire useful life u of the unit. At time t, then, where $v \leq t \leq v + u$, revenue from such a unit is $P(t)/b(v)$. Use (7) to write

$$(8) \qquad \frac{P(t)}{b(v)} = \frac{e^{q(t-v)}P(v)}{b(v)}$$

Let w be the money wage rate. Since one physical unit of producers' goods is by definition operated by one man, operating labor cost per physical unit of producers' goods is w. At time t, revenue *minus* operating labor cost is, then

$$(9) \qquad H(t) \equiv \frac{e^{q(t-v)}P(v)}{b(v)} - w$$

As seen from time v, revenue *minus* operating labor cost per small fraction dt of a year located at time t is $H(t)^{-r(t-v)}\,dt$, where r is the rate of interest. Define the gross worth as of time v of the new physical unit of producers' goods as discounted revenue *minus* operating labor cost over its entire useful life

$$(10) \qquad k(v) \equiv \int_{v}^{v+u} H(t)e^{-r(t-v)}\,dt$$

$$= \frac{P(v)}{b(v)} \frac{1 - e^{(q-r)u}}{r - q} - w\,\frac{1 - e^{-ru}}{r}$$

Assume the salvage value of the unit when retired to be zero. The net worth of a new physical unit of producers' goods of vintage v, as seen at time v, is defined as gross worth *minus* the price of the unit:

$$(11) \qquad n(v) \equiv k(v) - p$$

Insert (2) and (10) into (11) and express net worth

$$(12) \qquad n(v) = \frac{P(v)}{b(v)} \frac{1 - e^{(q-r)u}}{r - q} - w\,\frac{1 - e^{-ru} + ar}{r}$$

It follows from (5) and (7) that $P(t)/b(t) = P(v)/b(v)$. Consequently the price policy assumed by (7) will keep net worth (12) stationary to potential entrants to the consumers' goods industry and thus discourage entry.

5. Optimal Replacement

At time $t = v$ let our firm acquire $I(v) = b(v)X(v)$ new producers' goods just adequate to satisfy the demand faced by the firm at that time

$$(13) \qquad\qquad C(v) = X(v)$$

At time $t = v + u$ let the firm replace them by $I(v + u) = b(v + u)X(v)$ new producers' goods just adequate to maintain constant capacity. Why constant capacity? Our problem is a problem of pure replacement, hence should be purged of anything having to do with expansion. Now according to (5), $b(v + u) = e^{qu}b(v)$, where $q < 0$; consequently fewer new producers' goods are needed to maintain constant capacity: $I(v + u) = e^{qu}b(v)X(v)$.

At time $t = v + 2u$ the firm replaces by $I(v + 2u) = b(v + 2u)X(v)$ new producers' goods. Now still fewer new producers' goods are needed to maintain constant capacity: $I(v + 2u) = e^{2qu}b(v)X(v)$.

Every u years another replacement takes place, and at time $t = v + ju$ the jth replacement takes place: The firm replaces by $I(v + ju) = b(v + ju)X(v)$ new producers' goods, and $I(v + ju) = e^{jqu}b(v)X(v)$. Remembering that net worth of a new unit is stationary, $n(v) = n(v + ju)$, write the total net worth, as seen at time $t = v + ju$, of the jth replacement as

$$(14) \qquad\qquad n(v + ju)I(v + ju) = e^{jqu}b(v)n(v)X(v)$$

Let us see this net worth instead from time $t = v$. Discounting it from $t = v + ju$ to $t = v$ is accomplished by multiplying (14) by e^{-jru}, making it shrink to $e^{(q-r)ju}b(v)n(v)X(v)$. Now find the net worth, still as seen from $t = v$, of not only the jth replacement but of all the $j + 1$ successive generations $I(v), I(v + u), \ldots, I(v + ju)$. That net worth is

$$b(v)n(v)X(v)[1 + e^{(q-r)u} + e^{(q-r)2u} + \cdots + e^{(q-r)ju}]$$

The square bracket is a geometrical progression having $j + 1$ terms and the common ratio $e^{(q-r)u}$. Notice that the exponent $(q - r)u < 0$. Let j rise without bounds and find the net worth as seen from $t = v$ of such an endless series of generations $I(v), I(v + u), \ldots$ to be

$$J(v) \equiv \frac{b(v)n(v)X(v)}{1 - e^{(q-r)u}}$$

Insert (3), (12), and (13) and find

$$(15) \qquad J(v) = b(v)N(v)[P(v)]^{\eta}\left[\frac{P(v)}{b(v)}\frac{1}{r - q} - \frac{w}{r}\frac{1 - e^{-ru} + ar}{1 - e^{(q-r)u}}\right]$$

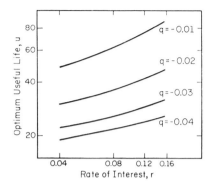

Figure 9-1. Mapping the replacement function (19), $a = 8$.

To maximize (15) take partial derivatives of $J(v)$ with respect to $P(v)$ and u. The first-order conditions for a maximum is that those partial derivatives are zero:

(16) $\quad \dfrac{\partial J(v)}{\partial P(v)} = b(v)N(v)[P(v)]^{\eta-1}\left[\dfrac{P(v)}{b(v)}\dfrac{1+\eta}{r-q} - \eta\,\dfrac{w}{r}\dfrac{1-e^{-ru}+ar}{1-e^{(q-r)u}}\right] = 0$

(17) $\quad \dfrac{\partial J(v)}{\partial u} = -b(v)N(v)[P(v)]^{\eta}\dfrac{w}{r}$

$$\times\ \dfrac{[1-e^{(q-r)u}]re^{-ru} + [1-e^{-ru}+ar](q-r)e^{(q-r)u}}{[1-e^{(q-r)u}]^2}$$

$$= 0$$

Solve (16) for $P(v)/b(v)$. Since in the solution all variables refer to the same time v, we purge it of v:

(18) $\qquad\qquad \dfrac{P}{b} = \dfrac{\eta}{1+\eta}\dfrac{r-q}{r}\dfrac{1-e^{-ru}+ar}{1-e^{(q-r)u}}\,w$

Solve (17) for u and find

(19) $\qquad\qquad re^{-qu} - qe^{-ru} = (1+ar)(r-q)$

Eq. (18) is an explicit solution for P/b. Eq. (19) is beautiful in its symmetry but does not permit an explicit solution for u. Consequently we have mapped it. A computer program[a] employing binary chopping and the Newton-Raphson method of approximating roots produced the data underlying Figure 9-1 and 9-2. We conclude that optimal useful life u is the longer the

---

[a] Written by Robert A. Meyer for an I.B.M. 7094 at the University of Illinois in 1964.

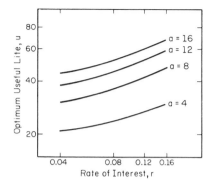

Figure 9-2. Mapping the replacement function (19), $q = -0.02$.

costlier are the producers' goods, the higher is the rate of interest, and the slower is the rate of technological progress. These three results make intuitive sense: The costlier the producers' goods and the higher the rate of interest, the more urgent it becomes to save capital cost by lengthening useful life. The slower the rate of technological progress, the lower the pressure for replacement.

For the purposes of the next chapter we shall find it useful to express P/b as a function of useful life u, so use (19) to express e^{-ru} in terms of e^{-qu}, multiply (19) by e^{qu} to express $e^{(q-r)u}$ in terms of e^{qu}, and insert the two results into (18). As a result, the latter collapses into

(20)
$$\frac{P}{b} = \frac{\eta}{1 + \eta} \, we^{-qu}$$

The appendix will prove that the second-order conditions for a maximum of Eq. (15) are satisfied.

Appendix: Second-order Conditions for a Maximum of Equation (15)

Write the Hessian

(21)
$$\begin{vmatrix} \dfrac{\partial^2 J}{\partial P^2} & \dfrac{\partial^2 J}{\partial P\,\partial u} \\[2ex] \dfrac{\partial^2 J}{\partial u\,\partial P} & \dfrac{\partial^2 J}{\partial u^2} \end{vmatrix}$$

The first derivatives of J with respect to P and u have already been found, i.e., (16) and (17). Use them to find the second derivatives entering the Hessian:

(22)
$$\frac{\partial^2 J}{\partial P^2} = NP^{n-1}\frac{1 + \eta}{r - q}$$

(23), (24)
$$\frac{\partial^2 J}{\partial P\,\partial u} = \frac{\partial^2 J}{\partial u\,\partial P} = 0$$

(25)
$$\frac{\partial^2 J}{\partial u^2} = bNP^n qwe^{-ru}$$

Under the assumptions made, all factors of (22) are positive except $1 + \eta$, which is negative, hence (22) is negative. All factors of (25) are positive except q, which is negative, hence (25) is negative. So the Hessian is positive. The principal minor formed by deleting last row and column is negative. Consequently the second-order conditions for a maximum are satisfied.

150

Notes

[1] Intriligator, M. D., "Embodied Technical Change and Productivity in the United States 1929–1958," *Rev. Econ. Stat.*, Feb. 1965, **47,** 65–70.

[2] Lydall, H. F., "Technical Progress in Australian Manufacturing," *Econ. Jour.*, Dec. 1968, **78,** 807–826.

10

Optimal Replacement in a Vintage Model of Growth

This chapter will examine the steady-state [8] growth of an economy of firms like the one just studied in Chapter 9. The economy produces two goods, a consumers' good whose quality doesn't change over time and a producers' good whose quality does. Households have a propensity to consume real wages equalling one, and a propensity to consume real profits less than one. There is a money capital market in which firms may borrow and savers lend at the rate of interest r. There is a labor force growing at the constant proportionate rate g.[a]

1. Notation

Variables

$C \equiv$ consumption
$f \equiv$ labor's share of national money income
$H \equiv$ revenue *minus* operating labor cost per physical unit of producers' goods
$h \equiv$ gross investment to gross output ratio
$\theta \equiv$ payout ratio
$I \equiv$ investment
$k \equiv$ present gross worth of a physical unit of producers' goods
$L_1 \equiv$ labor employed by producers' goods industry
$L_2 \equiv$ labor employed by consumers' goods industry
$n \equiv$ present net worth of a physical unit of producers' goods
$P \equiv$ price of consumers' goods
$p \equiv$ price of producers' goods
$r \equiv$ rate of interest
$S \equiv$ physical capital stock of producers' goods

---

[a] Our own vintage model does not have as much capital-labor substitution as do the models of Johansen [9], Massell [15], and Solow [16]. An earlier version of our own two-sector vintage model was published in [1] without knowledge of a one-sector vintage model [17] offering an otherwise quite similar determination of the equilibrium rate of interest.

$u \equiv$ useful life of producers' goods
$W \equiv$ wage bill
$X \equiv$ physical output of consumers' goods
$Y \equiv$ national money income
$\Upsilon \equiv$ gross output
$Z \equiv$ profits bill

Parameters

$a \equiv$ labor required to produce one physical unit of producers' goods
$b \equiv$ physical capital coefficient
$c_W \equiv$ propensity to consume real wage bill
$c_Z \equiv$ propensity to consume real profits bill
$\eta \equiv$ price elasticity of demand for consumers' goods
$F \equiv$ available labor force
$g \equiv$ proportionate rate of growth of labor force
$q \equiv$ proportionate rate of technological progress
$w \equiv$ money wage rate

All flow variables refer to the instantaneous rate of that variable measured on a per annum basis. The parameters listed are stationary except b and F, whose proportionate rates of growth q and g, respectively, are stationary.

The symbol v is a vintage coordinate applied to capital coefficients b, labor employed by the consumers' goods industry L_2, and output of consumers' goods X. Symbols t and τ are time coordinates. The symbol e is Euler's number, the base of natural logarithms.

2. Pure Competition

This chapter will use all equations of Chapter 9, hence will continue the numbering commenced there. But we shall assume competition to be pure: Let the price elasticity η approach *minus* infinity, so we may use the approximation

(26)
$$\frac{\eta}{1 + \eta} = 1$$

Insert (18) and (26) into (12) and see that $n(v) = 0$.

3. Physical Capital Stock

The physical capital stock in existence at time τ includes every physical unit of producers' goods produced from time $\tau - u$ to time τ, hence is a heterogeneous mass of objects, called by Maddison [14] "a fossilized history of technology." How can we measure it? How can we add spades and bulldozers? Eq. (6) defined a physical unit of producers' goods as the equipment operated by one man. Thus measured, the physical capital stock in existence at time τ is

$$(27) \qquad S(\tau) \equiv \int_{\tau - u}^{\tau} I(v)\, dv$$

Still measuring in accordance with (6), let physical output I of producers' goods be growing at a proportionate rate g:

$$(28) \qquad I(\tau) = e^{g(\tau - v)} I(v)$$

Insert (28) into (27), integrate, and purge of τ:

$$(29) \qquad S = \frac{1 - e^{-gu}}{g} I$$

Eq. (29) expresses physical capital stock S in terms of physical output I of producers' goods of the latest vintage. Since I is growing at the proportionate rate g, so is S.

4. Full Employment

Eq. (6) defined a physical unit of producers' goods as the equipment operated by one man. Take the integral of (6) from $\tau - u$ to τ, using (27) and (29), and find total labor employed by the consumers' goods industry at time τ

$$(30) \qquad \int_{\tau - u}^{\tau} L_2(v)\, dv \equiv \int_{\tau - u}^{\tau} I(v)\, dv = \frac{1 - e^{-gu}}{g} I(\tau)$$

Add (1) and (30) to find aggregate employment and let that equal available labor force:

$$(31) \qquad \left(a + \frac{1 - e^{-gu}}{g} \right) I = F$$

Consequently the proportionate rate g at which physical output I of producers' goods was assumed to be growing, must be the proportionate rate of growth of labor force F.

5. Output

Physical output of producers' goods is I. Multiply (2) by I and find the money value of the output of producers' goods

$$(32) \qquad pI = awI$$

which is growing at the proportionate rate g, too.

Rearrange (4), take the integral of it from $\tau - u$ to τ, using (5) and (28), and find the physical output of consumers' goods flowing from the entire capital stock in existence at time τ:

$$(33) \qquad \int_{\tau-u}^{\tau} X(v)\, dv \equiv \int_{\tau-u}^{\tau} \frac{I(v)}{b(v)}\, dv$$

$$= \int_{\tau-u}^{\tau} e^{-(g-q)(\tau-v)} \frac{I(\tau)}{b(\tau)}\, dv$$

$$= \frac{1 - e^{-(g-q)u}}{g - q} \frac{I(\tau)}{b(\tau)}$$

It follows from (5) and (28) that physical output of consumers' goods as expressed by (33) is growing at the proportionate rate $g - q$. Multiply (33) by $P(\tau)$, use (20) and (26), and find the money value of the output of consumers' goods

$$(34) \qquad P(\tau) \int_{\tau-u}^{\tau} X(v)\, dv = \frac{1 - e^{-(g-q)u}}{g - q} e^{-qu} wI(\tau)$$

The money value of the output of consumers' goods as expressed by (34) is growing at the proportionate rate g, i.e., less rapidly than did physical output. The reason for this difference is the steady price decline assumed by (7).

Now add the money values of the two outputs (32) and (34) and find gross output

$$(35) \qquad \Upsilon = \left[a + \frac{1 - e^{-(g-q)u}}{g - q} e^{-qu} \right] wI$$

6. The Gross Investment to Gross Output Ratio

Divide (32) by (35) and find the gross investment to gross output ratio

$$(36) \qquad h \equiv \frac{pI}{\Upsilon} = \frac{a(g - q)}{a(g - q) + [1 - e^{-(g-q)u}]e^{-qu}}$$

The gross investment to gross output ratio as expressed by (36) is a function of useful life u and hence—*via* (19) as mapped in Table 10-1 and Figure 10-1—a function of the rate of interest r. Tables 10-2 and 10-3 and Figure

Table 10-1. Useful Life u as Computed from Equation (19)

Developed Economy: $a = 8, q = -0.03$

r	u
0.04	23.4
0.08	26.4
0.12	29.8
0.16	33.2

Underdeveloped Economy: $a = 4, q = -0.02$

r	u
0.08	24.0
0.12	27.1
0.16	30.6

Table 10-2. Values of Parameters and Variables in a Developed Economy

$a = 8, g = 0.01, q = -0.03$

Ratio	Rate of Interest, r			
	0.04	0.08	0.12	0.16
$h(36)$	0.207	0.181	0.158	0.138
$\theta(45)$	0.809	0.830	0.857	0.874
$f(46)$	0.923	0.851	0.777	0.716
$c_z(50)$	0.762	0.907	0.920	0.950

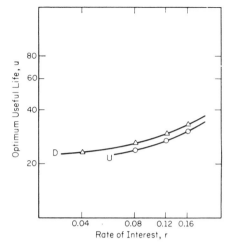

Figure 10-1. The replacement function (19) for developed and underdeveloped economies.

Table 10-3. Values of Parameters and Variables in an Underdeveloped Economy

$a = 4, g = 0.03, q = -0.02$

| Ratio | Rate of Interest, r | | |
	0.08	0.12	0.16
$h(36)$	0.150	0.136	0.122
$\theta(45)$	0.883	0.898	0.913
$f(46)$	0.899	0.851	0.800
$c_z(50)$	0.637	0.738	0.813

10-2 use empirically plausible values of the parameters a, g, and q. The tables and the figure show a high gross investment to gross output ratio h to go with a low rate of interest r.

So much for the output effect of the rate of interest. Now for the income and demand effect.

7. Gross Worth of a Used Physical Unit of Producers' Goods

Consider a physical unit of producers' goods of vintage v with a useful life u. At time t, where $v \leq t \leq v + u$, revenue *minus* operating labor cost is (9).

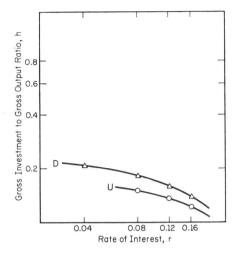

Figure 10-2. The gross investment to gross output ratio (36) in developed and underdeveloped economies.

As seen from time τ, where $v \leq \tau \leq v + u$, revenue *minus* operating labor cost per small fraction dt of a year located at time t is $H(t)e^{-r(t-\tau)} dt$. Define the gross worth as of time τ of the used physical unit of producers' good as discounted revenue *minus* operating labor cost over its remaining useful life:

$$(37) \qquad k(v, \tau) \equiv \int_{\tau}^{v+u} H(t)e^{-r(t-\tau)} dt$$

Insert (9), (20), and (26) and write gross worth

$$(38) \quad k(v, \tau) = \left[e^{-qu} \int_{\tau}^{v+u} e^{q(t-v)-r(t-\tau)} dt - \int_{\tau}^{v+u} e^{-r(t-\tau)} dt \right] w$$

$$= \frac{re^{-q(v+u-\tau)} - qe^{-r(v+u-\tau)} - (r-q)}{r(r-q)} w$$

8. Gross Worth of Capital Stock

What is the gross worth of all physical capital stock existing at time τ? Producers' goods of vintage v are produced at the rate $I(v)$. Producers' goods of vintages from v to $v + dv$, where dv is a small fraction of a year located at time v, are produced within that fraction of a year, hence their number at time τ is $I(v) \, dv$, and their gross worth as of time τ is $k(v, \tau)I(v) \, dv$. As seen at time τ the gross worth of producers' goods of all vintages existing at that time, i.e., of vintages $\tau - u$ through τ, is

$$(39) \qquad \int_{\tau-u}^{\tau} k(v, \tau)I(v) \, dv$$

Insert (28) and (38) into (39) and find

$$(40) \qquad \int_{\tau-u}^{\tau} k(v, \tau)I(v) \, dv = \frac{wI(\tau)}{r(r-q)} \int_{\tau-u}^{\tau} \left[re^{-q(v+u-\tau)+g(v-\tau)} \right.$$
$$\left. - \; qe^{-r(v+u-\tau)+g(v-\tau)} - (r-q)e^{g(v-\tau)} \right] dv$$
$$= \frac{wQI(\tau)}{r}$$

where

$$Q \equiv \frac{re^{-qu}}{(g-q)(r-q)} + \frac{qe^{-ru}}{(r-g)(r-q)} - \frac{qre^{-gu}}{g(g-q)(r-g)} - \frac{1}{g}$$

9. Profits Bill, Wage Bill, and National Money Income

Define [13] profits as interest on gross worth of capital stock. Multiply (40) by r and find the profits bill

$$(41) \qquad Z(\tau) \equiv r \int_{\tau-u}^{\tau} k(v, \tau)I(v) \, dv = wQI(\tau)$$

Use (31) to write the wage bill

$$(42) \qquad W \equiv wF = \left(a + \frac{1 - e^{-gu}}{g} \right) wI$$

Define national money income as the sum of the profits and wage bills. Add (41) and (42):

$$(43) \qquad Y \equiv Z + W = \left(Q + a + \frac{1 - e^{-gu}}{g} \right) wI$$

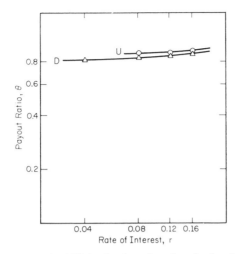

Figure 10-3. The payout ratio (45) in developed and underdeveloped economies.

Use (19) to express $qe^{-ru} = re^{-qu} - (1 + ar)(r - q)$, insert that into Q, insert Q into Y and write national money income as

(44) $$Y = \frac{re^{-qu} + (g - q - r)e^{-gu} - (1 + ag)(g - q)}{(g - q)(r - g)} \, wI$$

10. The Payout Ratio

Define[b] the payout ratio θ as the national money income to gross output ratio. Divide (44) by (35):

(45) $$\theta \equiv \frac{Y}{Y} = \frac{re^{-qu} + (g - q - r)e^{-gu} - (1 + ag)(g - q)}{\{a(g - q) + [1 - e^{-(g-q)u}]e^{-qu}\}(r - g)}$$

The payout ratio as expressed by (45) is a function of useful life u and hence—*via* (19) as mapped in Figure 10-1—a function of the rate of interest r. Tables 10-2 and 10-3 and Figure 10-3 show a low payout ratio θ to go with a low rate of interest r.

---

[b] The importance of the payout ratio was seen by Keynes [10], 98 and 104. The payout ratio should not be confused with the dividends-to-profits ratio of a corporation [2].

11. Labor's Share

Define labor's share as the wage bill to national money income ratio. Divide (42) by (44):

$$(46) \qquad f \equiv \frac{W}{Y} = \frac{(g - q)(r - g)[a + (1 - e^{-gu})/g]}{re^{-qu} + (g - q - r)e^{-gu} - (1 + ag)(g - q)}$$

Labor's share as expressed by (46) is a function of useful life u and hence—*via* (19) as mapped in Figure 10-1—a function of the rate of interest r. Tables 10-2 and 10-3 and Figure 10-4 show a high labor's share f to go with a low rate of interest r.

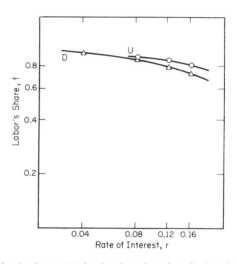

Figure 10-4. Labor's share (46) in developed and underdeveloped economies.

12. Consumption Demand

Let the propensity to consume real profits be less than the propensity to consume real wages, as Lindahl [13], 174, and the Cambridge, England school [8], 793–794, have insisted it should. Indeed let $0 < c_Z < 1$ and $c_W = 1$. Use (41) and (42) to write consumption demand

$$(47) \qquad C \equiv \frac{c_Z Z}{P} + \frac{c_W W}{P} = \left[c_Z Q + a + \frac{1 - e^{-gu}}{g} \right] \frac{wI}{P}$$

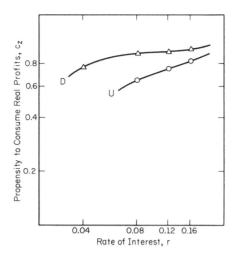

Figure 10-5. Propensity to consume real profits (50) in developed and under-developed economies.

13. Gross and Net Savings Ratios

Use our four definitions (43), (45), (46), and (47) with $c_W = 1$ inserted to find the gross and net savings ratios

(48) $$\frac{\Upsilon - PC}{\Upsilon} \equiv 1 - \theta[c_Z(1 - f) + f]$$

(49) $$\frac{Y - PC}{Y} \equiv 1 - [c_Z(1 - f) + f]$$

14. Equilibrium

As an equilibrium condition, equate physical output of consumers' goods (33) and consumption demand (47), insert (20) and (26), and express the propensity to consume real profits

(50) $$c_Z = \frac{[1 - e^{-(g-q)u}]e^{-qu}/(g - q) - [a + (1 - e^{-gu})/g]}{Q}$$

The propensity c_Z to consume real profits as expressed by (50) is a function of useful life u and hence—*via* (19) as mapped in Figure 10-1—a function of the rate of interest r. Tables 10-2 and 10-3 and Figure 10-5 show a low propensity c_Z to go with a low rate of interest r.

It may seem strange to "solve" for the parameter c_Z rather than for the rate of interest r. But (19) and (50) taken together would not permit an explicit solution for r. Still, (50) is the clue to a determination of the equilibrium rate of interest. We use it as follows.

On their right-hand sides our four ratios h (36), θ (45), f (46), and c_Z (50) contain nothing but, first, the three stationary parameters $a \equiv$ labor required to produce one physical unit of producers' goods; $g \equiv$ proportionate rate of growth of labor force; and $q \equiv$ proportionate rate of technological progress; second, Euler's number e; and third, the two variables $r \equiv$ rate of interest and $u \equiv$ useful life. Consequently, if the rate of interest r remains stationary, so does useful life u according to (19), so do the four ratios h, θ, f, and c_Z, and so do the gross and net savings ratios (48) and (49) defined solely in terms of θ, f, and c_Z.

This means once equilibrium, always equilibrium: Once we can find an equilibrium rate of interest r, we have found equilibrium forever! Can we?

Consider the case of a developed economy whose parameters are: $a = 8$; $c_Z = 0.907$; $g = 0.01$; and $q = -0.03$. To keep our four ratios h, θ, f, and c_Z in a stationary equilibrium would require a rate of interest $r = 0.08$: According to Table 10-2, such an interest rate would generate a gross investment to gross output ratio $h = 0.181$, a payout ratio $\theta = 0.830$, and a labor's share $f = 0.851$. As defined by (48) the gross savings ratio would then be 0.181. The gross investment and gross savings ratios would then be equal!

What if the rate of interest had been higher, say $r = 0.16$? According to Table 10-2 this would have reduced the gross investment to gross output ratio to $h = 0.138$, raised the payout ratio to $\theta = 0.874$, and reduced labor's share to $f = 0.716$. As defined by (48) the gross savings ratio would then have been 0.149. The gross investment and gross savings ratios would no longer have been equal! Eq. (50) and Table 10-2 can be used to see that their equality under such a high rate of interest would have required a higher c_Z, i.e., $c_Z = 0.950$.

What if the rate of interest had been lower, say $r = 0.04$? This would have raised the gross investment to gross output ratio to $h = 0.207$, reduced the payout ratio to $\theta = 0.809$, and raised labor's share to $f = 0.923$. The gross savings ratio would then have been 0.197—not equal to the gross investment ratio. Their equality at such a low rate of interest would have required a $c_Z = 0.762$!

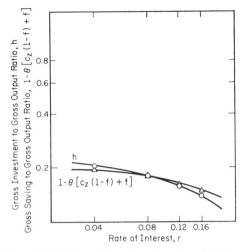

Figure 10-6. The savings-investment equilibrium.

Since a high rate of interest generated positive, and a low rate of interest negative, excess saving, our rate-of-interest equilibrium, shown in Figure 10-6, is a stable one.[c]

Similarly we could have shown that a stable rate-of-interest equilibrium would exist in an underdeveloped economy at $a = 4$; $c_z = 0.738$; $g = 0.03$; $r = 0.12$; and $q = -0.02$.

15. Conclusion: Labor's Benefit from Capital Quickening

Use (20) and (26) to write the real wage rate

$$(51) \qquad \frac{w}{P} = \frac{e^{qu}}{b}$$

Since the physical capital coefficient b was changing at the proportionate rate q, where $q < 0$, the real wage rate as expressed by (51) is growing at the

---

[c] Without considering useful life a function of the rate of interest, Eisner [5], [6] and Domar [4] found depreciation allowances to exceed replacement requirements in a growing economy. Defining a generalized drag as the excess of gross saving over gross investment, we have—by definition—a zero drag at our equilibrium rate of interest, a positive drag at a rate higher than that, and a negative drag at a rate lower than that, as shown in Figure 10-6.

proportionate rate $-q$. To the technologically determined rate q a low propensity c_Z to consume real profits, the resulting low rate of interest r, the resulting short useful life u, and capital quickening can contribute nothing. They can, however, contribute to the *level* of the real wage rate: At a given time, w/P as expressed by (51) is the higher the lower the useful life u, occurring in the numerator e^{qu}, for $q < 0$.

In addition, a low propensity c_Z to consume real profits, the resulting low rate of interest r, the resulting short useful life u, and capital quickening contribute to labor's share f—see Table 10-2!

Thus the Wicksell Effect [19] is operating under capital quickening no less than under capital deepening: "The capitalist saver is, thus, fundamentally, the friend of labour."

Appendix:
Empirical
Measurements

1. Empirically Plausible Ranges of a, g, and q

Write a as the identity $a \equiv awS(\tau)/[wS(\tau)]$, then use (2), (27), and (30) to write it $a = pS(\tau)/[w \int_{\tau-u}^{\tau} L_2(v)\, dv]$, or the ratio between the undepreciated value of capital stock and the consumers' goods industry's wage bill. In the real world, the producers' goods industry uses producers' goods, too, so let us look for the ratio between the undepreciated value of capital stock and the aggregate wage bill. In developed and underdeveloped economies, respectively, the undepreciated value of capital stock could be 6 and 3 times net national product, and labor's share $\frac{4}{5}$ and $\frac{3}{4}$, respectively. Consequently, a would be 8 and 4, respectively.

Take definitions (4) and (6) together and see that $b(v) \equiv L_2(v)/X(v)$ or the reciprocal of labor productivity in the consumers' goods industry. Ignore the fact that labor productivity rises faster in the consumers' than in the producers' goods industry and look for overall labor productivity. For 1950–1960 Maddison [14], 36–37, found the following proportionate rates of growth:

	United States	Average, 12 OECD Countries
Man hours worked	0.009	0.007
Output per man hour	0.024	0.035

The reciprocal of labor productivity was, then, growing at -0.024 and -0.035, respectively. As an approximation for a developed economy we use $g = 0.01$ and $q = -0.03$.

Kuznets [12], 440, estimated the proportionate rate of growth of population of the underdeveloped economies to be around 0.025. For 1950–1960 the United Nations [18], 37, estimated the proportionate rate of growth of the gross national product of the underdeveloped economies to be 0.044. For a sample of 31 underdeveloped economies in 1957–1962, Chenery and Strout [3], 684, found it to be 0.046. Assuming man hours per capita to have been stationary, we find labor productivity and its reciprocal to have been growing at the rates 0.020 and -0.020, respectively. As an approximation for an underdeveloped economy we use $g = 0.03$ and $q = -0.02$.

2. The Payout Ratio

At the equilibrium rate of interest $r = 0.08$ we found a payout ratio $\theta = 0.830$ for a developed economy. Is that plausible? Kuznets [12], 236–239 and 248–250, estimated gross domestic capital formation to gross national product ratios (our h) as well as capital consumption to gross domestic capital formation ratios. Multiplying the former and the latter yields capital consumption to gross national product ratios. Deduct the latter from one and find Kuznets values for our payout ratio θ in postwar United States:

1946–1955	0.885
1950–1959	0.906

Why does our model undershoot? Two discrepancies between our model and the real world offer explanations. First, Kuznets' real world has government, hence has in it indirect business tax and nontax liability and business transfer payments *less* net subsidies of government enterprises. Had we deducted all that to get from gross national product to national income, we would have found a considerably lower Kuznets payout ratio. But even what we did deduct may be too little: In our model the price of a new physical unit of producers' goods was stationary, hence there couldn't be any difference between depreciation allowances at original cost and at replacement cost. In the real world there is a very considerable difference. The United States Department of Commerce price deflator for gross fixed capital formation rose more than two and a half times from 1929 to 1959; yet the Department calculates depreciation allowances at original cost rather than replacement cost, thus understating depreciation allowances.

3. Labor's Share

At the equilibrium rate of interest $r = 0.08$ we found a labor's share $f = 0.851$ for a developed economy. Is that plausible? Dividing the income of noncorporate enterprise between labor and property income in the same proportion as that prevailing outside the noncorporate-enterprise sector, and using depreciation allowance at replacement cost rather than original cost, Kravis [11], 930, estimated labor's share of national income in the United States in 1957 to have been 0.837. Our own value is quite plausible, then!

4. Gross and Net Savings Ratios

At the equilibrium rates of interest $r = 0.08$ and $r = 0.12$ for a developed and an underdeveloped economy, respectively, our model offers the following values of gross and net savings ratios:

	Developed	Underdeveloped
Gross, $1 - \theta[c_z(1 - f) + f]$	0.181	0.136
Net, $1 - [c_z(1 - f) + f]$	0.013	0.037

Are those findings plausible? The gross savings ratio for a developed economy 0.181 is practically the same as the Kuznets values for postwar United States [12], 236–237:

1946–1955	0.182
1950–1959	0.184

The gross savings ratio for an underdeveloped economy, 0.136, is plausible, too: For 31 underdeveloped economies in 1957–1962, Chenery and Strout [3], 684, estimated a gross savings ratio of 0.12. But out net savings ratio 0.013 is much lower than the Kuznets values for postwar United States [12], 248–249:

1946–1955	0.098
1950–1959	0.098

We have already seen a possible explanation for this undershooting: The United States Department of Commerce calculates depreciation allowances at original cost rather than replacement cost, thus understating depreciation. But understating depreciation means overstating net income and classifying as net saving what should have been classified as depreciation allowances.

5. A Kuznets Question Answered

For the United States and the United Kingdom 1870–1960 Kuznets [12], 236–237 and 248–249 found gross and net saving behaving very differently: The gross savings ratio was rising in the United Kingdom and approximately stationary in the United States. By contrast, the net savings ratio showed a significant decline in both countries. This made Kuznets ask [12], 251:

... why have the [net savings] ratios declined or failed to rise in some countries, and why were they so low in others—all in periods of rather vigorous growth and marked rise in real income per capita?

Our own model may answer that question. Think of economic history as a slow switch from a capital-short, high-rate-of-interest, steady-state underdeveloped equilibrium towards a capital-abundant, low-rate-of-interest, steady-state developed equilibrium. Think of economic history as capital quickening! Such a switch began gathering momentum in England two hundred years ago; in the United States one hundred and fifty years ago; somewhat later in Germany; even later in Japan and Sweden.

We just saw that such a switch from an underdeveloped to a developed equilibrium would *raise* the gross savings ratio from 0.136 to 0.181 but *reduce* the net savings ratio from 0.037 to 0.013. Such switching simulates the Kuznets findings superbly!

6. Equilibrium Rates of Interest

Are our equilibrium rates of interest $r = 0.08$ and $r = 0.12$ for a developed and an underdeveloped economy, respectively, themselves plausible? Kuznets [12], 421, estimated the yield on all income-yielding material assets, including land, outside the equity of individual noncorporate enterprise to be 6.1 and 13 per cent, respectively, in developed and underdeveloped economies. Kravis [11], 938, using the procedure described in Section 3 of this appendix, estimated the rate of return on reproducible assets alone in the United States to be 0.09 per cent. Our equilibrium rates of interest, then, are plausible.

7. Money versus Physical Capital Coefficient

Multiply (29) by the price p of producers' goods, use (2), and find the undepreciated value of capital stock. Divide that by gross output Y as expressed by (35) and write our money gross capital coefficient:

$$(52) \qquad \frac{pS}{Y} = \frac{a(g - q)(1 - e^{-gu})/g}{a(g - q) + [1 - e^{-(g-q)u}]e^{-qu}}$$

For a stationary rate of interest r, useful life u and with it (52) will also remain stationary. Consequently, the steady decline in our physical capital coefficient $b(v)$ as defined by (5) is completely hidden! How come? The reason is the steady rise in the relative price of producers' goods: The price ratio p/P between producers' and consumers' goods is rising at the proportionate rate $-q$, where $q < 0$. Is such a price rise plausible? From 1929 to 1959 Gordon [7], 939, found the price ratio between producers' and consumers' goods in the United States to have increased by 0.013 per annum. This is only half our own value of $-q = 0.03$. The reason for the discrepancy is that in our model—but not in the real world—producers' goods are made from labor alone, hence do not benefit from technological progress themselves. According to Gordon [7], 948, it is true, however, that "taken as a whole, the capital goods sector is more labor-intensive than that for consumers' goods."

At the equilibrium rates of interest $r = 0.08$ and $r = 0.12$ for a developed and an underdeveloped economy, respectively, our model would offer the values 4.20 and 2.51 of (52), respectively. Are such values plausible? The gross domestic capital formation to incremental gross output ratio was estimated for the postwar United States by Kuznets [12], 254, at 4.7 and by Maddison [14], 77, at 5.8. For 31 underdeveloped economies in 1957–1962, Chenery and Strout [3], 684, found the ratio to be 3.52. Both our own values undershoot somewhat, then, but it remains true that the money gross capital coefficient is considerably higher in developed than in underdeveloped economies.

Notes

[1] Brems, H., *Quantitative Economic Theory*, New York, 1968, Ch. 48.

[2] Brittain, J. A., *Corporate Dividend Policy*, Washington, D.C., 1966.

[3] Chenery, H. B., and A. M. Strout, "Foreign Assistance and Economic Development," *Am. Econ. Rev.*, Sep. 1966, **56,** 679–733.

[4] Domar, E. D., "Depreciation, Replacement, and Growth," *Econ. Jour.*, Mar. 1953, **63,** 1–32.

[5] Eisner, R., "Depreciation Allowances, Replacement Requirements, and Growth," *Am. Econ. Rev.*, Dec. 1952, **42,** 820–831.

[6] Eisner, R., "Technological Change, Obsolescence, and Aggregate Demand," *Am. Econ. Rev.*, Mar. 1956, **46,** 92–105.

[7] Gordon, R. A., "Differential Changes in the Prices of Consumers' and Capital Goods," *Am. Econ. Rev.*, Dec. 1961, **51,** 937–957.

[8] Hahn, F. H., and R. C. O. Matthews, "The Theory of Economic Growth: A Survey," *Econ. Jour.*, Dec. 1964, **74,** 779–902.

[9] Johansen, L., "Substitution versus Fixed Production Coefficients in the Theory of Economic Growth: A Synthesis," *Econometrica*, Apr. 1959, **27,** 157–176.

[10] Keynes, J. M., *The General Theory of Employment, Interest, and Money*, London, 1936, 98, 104.

[11] Kravis, I. B., "Relative Income Shares in Fact and Theory," *Am. Econ. Rev.*, Dec. 1959, **49,** 917–949.

[12] Kuznets, S., *Modern Economic Growth, Rate, Structure, and Spread*, New Haven and London, 1966.

[13] Lindahl, E., *Studies in the Theory of Money and Capital*, London, 1939, 99–101, 143–146.

[14] Maddison, A., *Economic Growth in the West*, New York, 1964.

[15] Massell, B. F., "Investment, Innovation, and Growth," *Econometrica*, Apr. 1962, **30,** 239–252.

[16] Solow, R. M., "Investment and Technical Progress," K. J. Arrow et al. (eds.), *Mathematical Models in the Social Sciences*, Stanford, 1960.

[17] Solow, R. M., J. Tobin, C. C. von Weizsäcker, and M. Yaari, "Neo-classical Growth with Fixed Factor Proportions," *Rev. Econ. Stud.*, Apr. 1966, **33,** (2), 79–115.

[18] United Nations, *World Economic Survey* 1963, Part I, New York, 1964.

[19] Wicksell, K., *Lectures on Political Economy, I*, London, 1934, 164.

172

Epilogue

This book has been an exercise in steady-state growth—balanced or unbalanced. It has lately become fashionable to deny the feasibility of steady-state growth. Instead imminent doom is being preached [1], resulting from (a) the constancy of nonexhaustible nature, (b) the exhaustion of exhaustible nature, and (c) pollution.

As for the constancy of nonexhaustible nature, our Chapter 5, Section V, 4 found steady-state growth to be in no way precluded by such constancy: Output and capital stock would eventually be growing at the same steady-state proportionate rate. That rate might be lower than when nature was ignored, but it was still a steady-state rate. We did find that if the natural-resource elasticity of output was high enough, if labor-force growth was high enough, or if technological progress was low enough, the economy could generate a decaying real wage rate.

As for the exhaustion of exhaustible nature—not touched upon in the present book—such exhaustion may be a physical fact, but a physical fact may well lack economic significance. If an economy is running out of vital exhaustible resources, a necessary symptom would be rising relative prices of such resources. Of such a rise there is as yet no general evidence—quite the contrary: Primary producers seem to be victims of worsening terms of trade! Consequently, either we aren't running out or, if we are, the resources aren't vital but have been rendered superfluous by technological progress.

Pollution—not touched upon in the present book either—is a problem whose solution would seem to lie in making the polluters pay for their pollution, thus giving technological progress an incentive to come up with nonpolluting, less polluting, or pollution-neutralizing processes.

How, then, do the doomsday preachers generate their imminent doom? Simply by always visualizing technological progress as a once-and-for-all event: "We doubled the resource reserves in 1900" [1], 127; "We ... assumed that, starting in 1975, programs of reclamation and recycling will reduce the input of virgin resources needed per unit of industrial output to only one-fourth of the amount used today" [1], 133; "Assuming ... a reduction in pollution generation from all sources by a factor of four, starting in 1975" [1], 135; "We assume that the normal yield per hectare of all the world's land can be further increased by a factor of two" [1], 139. It is surprising that System Dynamics should have relied on such a static view of technological progress.

Much more realistically, this book has always visualized technology as progressing exponentially: Technological progress is itself steady-state

173

growth! In seeing no imminent doom, this book is in agreement with some of the best professional opinion [2] seeing, instead, a high elasticity of substitution between natural resources and other inputs and seeing continued scope for technological progress.

Notes

[1] Meadows, D. H., D. L. Meadows, J. Randers, and W. W. Behrens III, *The Limits to Growth, A Report for the Club of Rome's Project on the Predicament of Mankind*, New York, 1972.

[2] Nordhaus, W., and J. Tobin, "Is Growth Obsolete?" *Fiftieth Anniversary Colloquium V by the National Bureau of Economic Research*, New York, 1972, 1–80.

175

Index

Index

About the Author

Hans Brems was born in Denmark in 1915, is a Ph.D. of the University of Copenhagen (1950), taught at Berkeley from 1951 to 1954, and came to the University of Illinois in 1954.

At home Professor Brems has taught as visiting professor at U.C.L.A. (1953), Michigan (1957), Berkeley (1959), Harvard (1960), and the University of Colorado (1963).

Abroad he has taught courses on growth and cycles at Kiel (1961), on growth and international trade at Göttingen (1964), on general equilibrium and capital theory at Hamburg (1967), on two-country growth models at Uppsala (1968), on the Old and the New in capital theory at Lund (1970), on international economics at the Swedish School of Economics at Helsinki (1968 and 1970). In 1970 the latter institution awarded him an honorary doctor's degree. Furthermore, he taught the theory of labor, capital, and growth at Kiel (1972) and at Göteborg (1972).

In the March-April 1972 issue of the *Journal of Political Economy*, L. Hansen and B. Weisbrod published a survey of articles in journals indexed in the Index of Economic Journals. In award V, most total articles per year, based on 21 or more lifetime articles, 1886–1965, Brems was included among the top ten authors.

Previous Books by the Author

Product Equilibrium under Monopolistic Competition (Harvard 1951), *Output, Employment, Capital, and Growth* (Harper 1959), *Quantitative Economic Theory* (Wiley 1968), *Økonomiske langtidsperspektiver* (Sparevirke, Copenhagen 1971).